Benjamin Franklin Taylor

Old-time pictures and sheaves of rhyme

Benjamin Franklin Taylor

Old-time pictures and sheaves of rhyme

ISBN/EAN: 9783337259433

Printed in Europe, USA, Canada, Australia, Japan

Cover: Foto ©Thomas Meinert / pixelio.de

More available books at **www.hansebooks.com**

OLD-TIME PICTURES

AND

SHEAVES OF RHYME.

BY

Author of "JANUARY AND JUNE," "LIFE AND SCENES IN THE ARMY," etc

SECOND EDITION.

CHICAGO:
S. C. GRIGGS & COMPANY,
1874.

Entered, according to Act of Congress, in the year 1873, by
S. C. GRIGGS & COMPANY,
in the office of the Librarian of Congress, at Washington.

June Seventh,
1852.

TO HER FOR WHOM TWENTY YEARS HAVE NOT DIMMED THE
MEMORY OF THAT LONG-GONE DAY, THIS
LITTLE BOOK IS

Most Affectionately Inscribed.

PREFACE.

SET adrift in the newspapers, like thistle-down in the Fall wind, a few poems of mine have "lodged" at last between the lids of a book.

Never thinking seriously about it until it was too late to think at all, I find myself fearing that their meaning to me is a sort of personal property I cannot make over to anybody, and that I should have slipped them in among the leaves of the Family Record, between the book of Malachi and the Gospel according to St. Matthew, as being the very place in a world of sinners about the safest from perusal.

A friend once sent me some withered pansies, but he brightened and humanized the faded things by writing a single line: "From the grave of Hamlet,

Prince of Denmark." Ah, how beautiful they turned, and what treasures they became!

Less fortunate than the pansies, this sheaf of rhymes has nobody to write the single line. Only this: I suspect one or two of them of being better than I once thought, because several clever people have stolen and never returned them.

THE SHEAF.

	PAGE.
An Old-Time Picture	13
The Child and the Star	38
Thanksgiving	52
A Poet's Legacy	56
The Song of the Age	61
June	63
October	74
Tornado Sunday	78
The Skylark	82
Bunker Hill	87
The Old Village Choir	89
Going Home	92
The Dead Grenadier	97
Rhymes of the River	102
Lazy	109
Dearborn Observatory	112
Jenny June	115
Burns' Century Song	118
The Colored Marble	122
Flowers	123

	PAGE.
THE NEW CRAFT IN THE OFFING	124
THE VANE ON THE SPIRE	127
DECORATION DAY	132
A WINTER PSALM	135
SAILING OF COLUMBUS	141
THE CHRYSALIS	142
THE FLAG	143
THE HERO OF NEW HAMBURG	144
THE GOSPEL OF THE OAK	151
THE TWO JOHNS	154
BEAUTIFUL "MAY"	158
THE NORTHERN LIGHTS	160
INDIAN SUMMER	161
THE SHATTERED RAINBOW	162
FIRE AND WATER	163
"ATLANTIC"	167
CAVALRY CHARGE	174
FORT DEARBORN	176
THE ISLE OF THE LONG AGO	188
THE ROSE AND THE ROBIN	191

AN OLD-TIME PICTURE.

JULY 4TH, 1776 — JULY 4TH, 1873.

LET us roll back the world on its axle of fire,
Let us halt, if we can, just a breath or two nigher
The sweet simple time when they halved every trouble,
Ere pinks were carnations and roses all double!

We will watch for a roof with a slope down behind,
Like a sun-bonnet blown partly off by the wind,
Till the tresses of brown turn to gold one by one,
As they shake out of shadow and shine in the sun —

For a chimney as broad as the curb of a well
Where the ember-red maple leaves eddied and fell,
That volcanic plumed up with its volumes of smoke
That were crimson and gold when day brightened and broke; —

For a neighborly porch with the brow of a Greek
That will make you as welcome as if it could speak,
With a vine that runs up like a creature alive,
And as brisk as a bee that is bound from the hive
It goes rambling about with inquisitive leaves,
And then swings in a frolic along the low eaves ; —

For a rusty-gray curb, round a rugged stone well,
Where with dangle of bucket the sweep rose and fell
O'er the disc of still water, a silent black eye
That unsleeping, unwinking, is watching the sky ;
Now a star shines along, drops a beam down below,
Now a drift of noon cloud sheds a fleck of its snow,
Now a shadowy face smiling up to the brink
Where a girl smiling down has forgotten to drink ; —

For the hives of a fashion quaint, classic, and old.
Where the bees went and came with their burdens of gold —
'T was an African village of straw-woven cones
Within humming range of those myrtle-draped stones,

Of two borders of pinks, Sweet Williams and
    thyme,
That led out to the gate like a couplet in rhyme,—
Of the pæony's glow and the prince's own feather—
Of the four-o'clocks timing the dullest of weather,
Of the meek little asters, Earth's studies for stars,
And the love-lies-a-bleeding there close by the
    bars,—
Of the languid white poppy the dream-angels keep,
With its quaint-covered cup of the powder of
    sleep.
And sunflower and hollyhock, stately and tall,
And the cluster of lilacs beside the gray wall,
And the daffodils, columbines, roses, and all
That were kindred of Eve's without sinning at
    all;—

For the flinty old fields where the vicious-edged
    hoe
Always struck out a weed and a spark at a blow;—
For the pastures where mulleins and butter-cups
    grew,
And the white-legged sheep gnawed the summer
    all through;—

For a fringe of deep woods with a sugar-camp in it,
And the memories sweet as the song of a linnet;
And the drum of the partridge can summon my soul,
Like the drum of a drummer-boy beating the roll;
Ah, the thought of the " red-bird's " small flicker of fire
Can yet startle my pulses and kindle desire,—
And the green, plashy place where the slim rushes grew,
And the pendulum reeds, when the summer winds blew,
Set the bird with an epaulette swaying and swinging
'Till the bobolink's bells fell to rocking and ringing!
Ah, the fire of the camp as it threaded the trees,
And the smoke like a canopy swung by the breeze,
And the young moons of April and young girls of old,
How they flock to the heart like the lambs to the fold;
Ah, the dainty white flowers with their feet in the loam,
And as clean as an angel a minute from home!—

For the strawberry meadow so haunted with bees,
Where the boys and the girls crept about on their
  knees
And became — of each other — devout devotees;
Where the monarchs of twilight for ages had stood
And pronounced benediction with branches abroad,
Hark, the stroke of an axe like the tick of a clock:
  There's a burst of broad sunshine, a crushing of
    flowers;
Hark, the crash of the giants with shiver and shock:
  There's the chime of the wilderness striking the
    hours!
Lo, their monuments here that the mowers mow
  round
With a glint of the scythes that are rasping the
  ground; —

For the quilt of a field where the cradlers went in,
And their free swinging sweep seemed as easy as
  sin;
On the skeleton fingers the grain was laid down
Like the Babes in the Wood, far away from the
  town,

B

And the rakers and binders came rollicking after,
With their heads thatched with straw and their
    hearts full of laughter —
And perhaps the old farmer of Pomfret is one,
With a ring to his jokes like the flash of his gun;
And perhaps Molly Stark shades her eyes with
    her hand,
As she watches the boys that are sweeping the
    land; —

For a sky-line that rises and falls like the deep,
Lies as light on the hills with its tremulous sweep
As a mantle of blue on an infant asleep!

And the watch is all over — the picture is given,
And the scene is ringed in with a scollop of heaven.

The wide door on the latch opening full to the
    south
Is as sweet as the smile of an eloquent mouth.
When you swing on its hinges that neighborly door
A broad carpet of sunshine unrolls on the floor,
And a bee and a butterfly, freed from the fold —
And they must have been in it before it was rolled —

Like two figures escaped from a tapestry loom,
Are just drifting about in the rambling old room.

There's a touch of green caraway charming the air,
There's a low, loving ceiling, with a hook here and there,
Whence festoons of dried apples and pumpkins have hung
That the "bees" in checked aprons had quartered and strung;
There's a spotless white table, a broad open palm,
That has grown with the mouths like the swell of a psalm —
'T is a small hand of Providence, laden and spread,
That has answered the prayer of three ages for bread!

There's a thrush on the linden, a goldfinch adrift,
And a lark going up on a musical lift;
There's a girl in the garden, a "fellow" to love her,
And a robin in song in the maple above her;
There's a tin horn in tether adorning the wall,
And its twang, sharp and nasal, is sweeter than all!

AN OLD-TIME PICTURE.

There's a box on the window-sill, awkward and square,
"Live-forever" defiant is clustering there:
Ah, the *true* "live-forevers" are haunting the place,
And are thronging my soul with ineffable grace.

Let us rummage the drawers and the desolate "till"
For the snowy white cap, like a lily in frill,
And the string of gold dew-drops that beaded a neck,
And a bit of a dress in the blue and white check,
And the scolloped vandyke that the grandmothers wore,
And the short-gown and petticoat never seen more,
And the green silk calash, like the top of a chaise,
They could throw back at will in the dull, cloudy days
And then lift it again when the sky was a-blaze;
And the faded red "sampler," the work of Jane Ann,—
You can see with your heart how the alphabet ran—

AN OLD-TIME PICTURE.

And the year and *her* year: "'39,—age eleven,
And no older to-day, for she went young to
    Heaven!

The old room has grown human in all the long
    years —
Has been brightened by happiness, hallowed by
    tears;
By the brides on the hearth who will bless it no
    more,
By the cradles kept rocking like boats on the shore.
And that old-fashioned hearth with a flare to the
    jamb,
And a throat full of midnight to swallow the flame,
And a crane, like a witch's long slender black
    tongue,
In the yawn of red fire horizontally swung;
And a brace of tough fire-dogs, their feet in the
    coals,
Looking out from beneath the broad volume that
    rolls
Like the burst of a sunset in glory and gold,
That the touch of no Titian could ever have told.

Ah, the Arctic old hearts are alive that remember
All that splendor of fire in the perished December,
And the flicker and flash of the musketry rattle
When the hemlock and birch blazed away in sham battle,
And the sturdier glow of the hickory bank,
Reinforced with rock-maple in front and in flank,
When the surges rolled up and the rubies dropped down
Like the gems that are struck from a conquered king's crown,
Till the rush-bottomed chairs falling back in good order,
As the leaves flush apart in a wild rose's border,
All around the horizon the cider and song,
And the Baldwins and Greenings went circling along,
And the touching of hands and the whisper aside,
All the charms that survived it when Paradise died!
With the thought of that ingleside Eden is near,
Long deserted and cozy old corners of cheer!

See the jambs worn away by the shovel and tongs,
As the marble at Mecca was kissed by the throngs

That just pressed their live lips to the lips of the
 stone
'Till marble with mortal had blended and gone.
Ah, those long iron fingers to handle the fire
Were not made by the maker of Amphion's lyre,
But the sturdy old smith at the forks of the road
Smote them out of the bar as it sparkled and
 glowed,
Like the besom of Lucifer flourished the brand
'Till he swept out the dark with his angry right
 hand,—
And the kiss of the sledges fell fiercely and fast,
And the fingers were fashioned and finished at last;
With a sigh of relief they were plunged in the
 water,
And the tongs were baptized rough Vulcan's rude
 daughter.
Ah, the print of his hammer is plainer to-day
Than his name that they graved on a tablet of gray!

There's the ghost of a clock, with its body all gone,
Where it stood in a corner so ghastly and wan,
With a pallor of face that so haunted the wall
You felt like enshrouding the shape in a pall.

It was wound with a string, and its shadowy beat
Fell a faint and deliberate vision of feet.
How it marched through the night with an echo-
    less tread,
Like unshrived and unshodden impenitent dead!

On the mantel two candlesticks, iron and old,
That have lifted their glimmer long winters untold.
Ah, the slender white shafts, with their finish of
    flame,
That were lighted by those that old monuments
    name,
And the snuffers served up on a salver of tin,
When the crickets came out and the neighbors
    came in!

On the wall hangs the almanac, ledger of time,—
At the tail of each page is a ringlet of rhyme,
At the top is the sun, with a flare to his hair,
And the moon, from the shield to the sickle, is
    there,
And along the brief column's zodiacal blaze
Is the roll of the age's battalion of days

AN OLD-TIME PICTURE.

On the stand lies the Bible, that Day-Book so broad
It embodies the reckoning of mortals with God.
When the last of fourteen — just the lines in a son-
    net! —
  Is first seated at table, a twenty-pound man,
They just swing down the Book and enthrone him
    upon it,
And it brings him in range with the platter and
    pan.
On its cover the razor is cautiously strapped,
And within it the route of old Moses is mapped,
With the noblest of Sermons and sweetest of
    Psalms,
And the greenest of cedars and grandest of palms,
While Saint Matthew and Malachi guard the old
    story
Of the son that was born and the sire gone to glory —
Of the twain that were one, with an altar above it —
Of the darling that died, with a willow to love it;
'Tis the Blotter of tears for the mother and wife,
And belongs to the Ledger and Day-Book of Life!

On the gnarled wooden hooks, over mantle and all,
Is a battered Queen's Arm at a trail on the wall;

And that filbert-brown gun Saratoga has heard;
It has come to the shoulder at WASHINGTON'S word —
What was saucy to kings is as dumb as a sword!

In the blessed home-room, and that dreamy June day,
On the hearth were two children together at play:
One, a shrivelled gray man, shrunk away in his wear,
One, a boy like a distaff, with tow for his hair;
And one brought as he could the dead embers together,
And one blew for his life like a blast of March weather.
But the grizzled old boy was a-shiver in June,
And his mate's puckered lips sadly lacking a tune.

> He never heard the birds outside,
> He never felt the drifting tide
> Of song and fragrance mingled so,
> As strangely blent they float along,
> You think you *hear* the roses blow,
> And *smell* the robin's scented song.

Ah, the pulse that is dull with a dying desire
Can be warmed never more by an old kitchen fire!
But the shrivelled gray man dreamed his way back
    to life;
In the howl of December he heard the wild strife,
When the grand ragged regiments stood to the
    shock,
And the troopers came down like the wave on the
    rock.
So all things around helped his dreaming along,
And they rallied his heart like young Hopkinson's
    song.
E'en a kettle of samp that was lazily swung
On a hook's smutty finger, contentedly hung,
With its bubbles of gold, as they shattered and
    broke,
Made him think of the far-away musketry smoke,
When the field was red-edged with the troopers'
    red drift,
Like a border of cloud with a ray in the rift,
And the Georges in surges of scarlet did run
Like a line of shore-billows pursued by the sun!
And the lift of the lid at the touch of the steam
Was as measured and slow as a drum in a dream!

Of the boys on the hearth one was yet on his knees,
When the calm ruffled up with a breath of a breeze,
And a posy of girls blossomed into the room,
All the threads of their talk like the woof in a loom.
The old man looked round in a querulous way
On the exquisite grouping, as if he should say,
"Don't you s-e-e?— Here I am, in my ninetieth year!'
And he hollowed his hand till it fitted his ear.
"Oh, my grandfather dear," cried a willowy girl,—
And a pair of forefingers nimbly ran up a curl—
"I was saying 'next week is the FOURTH OF JULY.'"
Then the faded gray eye had a dawn like the sky,
Then the drowsy old heart gave an audible knock,
And he said, "I will pick the old flint in the lock—
"Ah, she never missed fire—there's a spark in her yet,
"And the rattling old talk she can never forget!"
Then the poor bended figure grew stately and tall,
For again he was hearing the bugler's old call;

The one hand was uplifted, the other was laid
On the thistle-down head with whom he had
    played,
And he murmured, "My boy, in whatever you do
"Be as right and as ready — the gun is for you —
"She's a quick-witted jade, but she's trusty and
    true."
Then a hush like a ghost that is here without
    coming,
Set the hearts of the maidens all halting and
    drumming,
And the breeze held its breath that was filling the
    room.
'T was as if one had spoken direct from the tomb,
With no charnel to rend and no coffin to rive,
And the First Resurrection had found them alive!

And the day broke at last, with its bunting and
    thunder,
And the eyes of the Thistle-down rounded with
    wonder;
A big anvil was pounding away in the road,
From the ridge of the barn a red banneret flowed;

On the pine in the yard perched an eagle benighted,
By a hand-breadth of stars in blue calico lighted.
And the "trainers" went by in white legs and blue breasts,
All their plumes tall and straight, and with blood on their crests,
And the riflemen green, in their fringes and frocks,
"Shutting pan" down the line like the ticking of clocks;
And the troopers rode on in fierce coat and fur frown
That had covered a bear, till it burdened them down.

With the ruffle and roll of the double drum corps,
And the fifes warbling up in the rumble and roar,
Like a bird half bewildered caught out in a storm,
Lo, there stood on the threshold the shrivelled gray form,
With the battered Queen's Arm — ah, the darling old girl!
And then, just as the wind blew the flag out of furl,

AN OLD-TIME PICTURE.

He was up with the musket and rattling away:
It was three and three more for the Deed and the
    Day,
And three rounds for the comrades that lay where
    they fell,
In the front of the battle, the border of hell;
And three guns for the Flag, and a toll for the dead
Old Commander who rode in the tempest and said,
"Blaze away there, my men! Are you *saving* your
    lead?"
So the clock struck thirteen—'twas an old-time
    salute,
And the smoke rolled away, and the musket was
    mute.

And the shadows were traveling eastwardly all,
They were shed from the trees in a lengthening
    fall,
They were reaching so lovingly over the land,
And were waving so strange when the forests
    were fanned,
You would fancy them fingers of pitiful Night,
That were gleaning the fields for a handful of light;

And they lay like a hand on the Veteran's head,
And he sat in his chair till the heavens were red,
And the musket and Thistle-down lay at his feet,
And his years were in sheaf like a bundle of wheat;
He had grounded his arms, and the Soldier was
    dead!

Ah, the world never halted, but trampled right
    on —
Not so much as a pansy for him that had gone,
And the grasses grew rank and the tablet grew
    small
Till the name on the stone had no meaning at all,
And the FOURTH OF JULY yet revolved like the
    Light
As it flashes to sea, intermitting the night.

There was growling of thunder low down in the
    sky,
And the crown of calamity lifted on high,
Every thorn was crushed home upon Liberty's
    brow —
Valley Forge's own imprint had bloodied its snow!

AN OLD-TIME PICTURE.

Then the trumpet of rally! The terrible tramp!
The blue skies had all fallen! The world was a
  camp!
Then the columns spread wide like the limbs of a
  larch,
And grew grander and broader. The world was
  a-march!
Then the crashing of cannon as batteries wheeled,
And the shock of the legions! The world was
  a-field!
And the bullets flew fiercer and farther and faster
In the storm equinoctial of death and disaster,
Till the gardens of Eden were mantled in gloom
And the world was a Ramah and Rachel at home!

And again it was June. The porch door was
  swung wide,
And the sunshine rolled in with a wonderful tide
Of the breath of the birds and the blossoms outside.
Framed by threshold and lintel, a picture of grace,
Stood a model of manhood, his heart in his face;
And the fellow was made on an exquisite plan,
With the eye of a woman, the mouth of a man;

And his mother stood near in white apron and arm—
And her silver-white hair did her beauty no harm—
With a wide maple bowl where she patted and rolled
With a broad wooden ladle an ingot of gold,
And then lifted the ball to a platter of delf;
It was Thistle-down's mother and Thistle-down's self!
While her locks were turned white, his were deep'ning to brown —

Then she nervously said, "What's the news from the town?"
"Oh, my mother," he cried, "there's a call for more men!
"And they've made it before — I can't *hear* it again!
"And no more 't would mean *me* had they called out my name!"
And his eyes were in tears, though his cheeks were aflame.

"Did they *lie* when they said that a man-child was born?
"It could never be *me*, and I hid in the corn! —

"All the boys march by bugle, and I by that horn!"
And he turned back a thumb at the pitiful thing,
Where it hung to the wall by its halter of string —
"Oh, my mother, say 'yes,'" and he bent low above her,
And he swallowed his heart like a pleading young lover;
"Do you mind of that FOURTH in old grandfather's time!
"'T was the half of a couplet — I'll *finish* the rhyme."
Then she lifted her face with a shiver of pain,
For the surge from her heart had rolled back from her brain,
And she said, "The Lord gave, and —" "Oh, no," he broke in,
"Let the sentence be ended right where you begin.
"Oh, not 'taken away' but just *borrowed* awhile;"
And then murmuring low, with a far-away smile,
"I'll come back in the blue, and we'll bless Him together,
"And we'll talk it all over, — this dark heavy weather.

"I will go — it is duty — the way the thing looks;"
And he took down the gun from the brown wooden hooks,
And he said, "I WILL KEEP MY OLD GRANDFATHER'S FOURTH!"
And he blent with the blue of the broad azure North.

Then the June came again, and the bee and the bird,
And the Thistle-down too, but he uttered no word,
Though he came in the blue, as he said he would come,
But with wailing of fife and the moaning of drum.

And the mother sat still in the sunny old porch,
And her eyes had burned down like a perishing torch,
But she took up the verse at the very same word:
"And has taken away, and be blessèd the Lord!"

AN OLD-TIME PICTURE.

Do you think that the FOURTH OF JULY can go down
While a Thistle-blow lives long enough to be brown?
It will yet be a child at an hundred years old!
Lo! the columns of Centuries grandly unfold!
Rear rank, open order! and front rank, about face!
And the Ages salute as they stand in their place,
And the DAY passes through with an eloquent grace!
See it shine down the lines with unquenchable light —
Good morn, Boy in Blue! Continental, GOOD NIGHT!

THE CHILD AND THE STAR.

OH, feel in your bosom, my darling,
    If the flutter is there as of old,
The pant of Sterne's captive, the starling,
    When this old-fashioned story is told.
Oh, the days sparkling up to the rim
    That bounds the one world by the other!
Oh, your heart even full to the brim
    With love like the love of your mother!
When you knew nothing more about sorrow or sin
Than the buttercups knew that she held to your
    chin,
While she watched with a smile your small secret
    unfold,
As it tinted the white with a glimmer of gold!

    We stood in the pasture together
        With the clover-breath over our heads,
    Right down from the Lord came the weather,
        Right up went the larks from their beds;

And we longed for a goldfinch's billow
  As it rode the invisible flood —
An oriole swung from a willow,
  And the daisies were bowing to God!
But the year was a harp, and like David the king's,
And the graver the cadence the longer the strings —
One by one went the days, growing briefer and fewer,
And we told them all off, and no tale could be truer, —
So we watched out the time with no thought of a sigh,
For our hearts danced and sang, "Merry Christmas is nigh!"

Oh, honey-bee, gypsy of summer,
  There's a flower that is sweeter than thine!
For thee there's an Angel for comer,
  With the sweep of a pinion divine.
Oh, Day on the hem of December!
  And oh, Star of old Bethlehem's brood!
Shine down in my heart like an ember
  With a glow from the altar of God.

Oh, fairest of flowers in the garden
    That dost blossom the brightest and last,
When our Eden has furloughed its warden,
    And the roses and lilies are past;
When Euroclydon's fingers so sculpture the snow,
That you hardly can tell if the sleeper below
Is just waiting for Spring, or the Trumpet to blow;
When the marble in motion and the Parian blend,
'Till the sexton must say where "God's acre" should end,
And 'mid these from the quarry and those from the cloud,
Must declare which they are that are wearing a shroud!

    Sit here by my side like a lover,
        Let us turn down the flare of the lamp,
    And talk the dear story all over
        'Till around us the shadows encamp.
    As we did in the days of the olden,
        We will light a dim candle again.
    For the blaze of a chandelier golden
        Never shone from the Now to the Then.

We will blow a dull coal to its glowing,
    As we blew it long ages ago,
While the Lord of the Harvest is sowing
    With His tempest out there in the snow.

Do you see that gray roof, strangely drifted with
    leaves,
And the moss all along on its low northern eaves?
'Tis as if Robin Redbreast, on duty again,
Would have covered my dead from the vision of
    men.
Each side of the gate a bold Lombardy stands,
As stately as warders, as graceful as wands,
That I watched long ago, while they swept the
    blue sky
All clear of the clouds that were loitering by!
I there in my cradle slowly rocking and dream-
    ing,
They clearing the road where the angels were
    gleaming.
Now I pause on the threshold the loving feet trod
That have walked upon thorns, that have gone up
    to God —

All traced here and there on threshold or stair
But the one pair that left not a print anywhere —
Ah, the little bare feet that had never been shod!

  Oh, heart of the house, my dead Mother,
    Give your boy the old greeting once more
  That I never have heard from another
    Since Death was let in at the door.
  I can reach up my hand to the ceiling
    Of the rooms once the world's greater part —
  Who wonders I cannot help feeling
    They have narrowed to fit to my heart!

Ah, these little green panes let the morning in late
But it never was stained by the emerald gate —
And the clock has run down in its desolate place, —
How we counted it in with its moon of a face,
When we said "Four were born but the *clock* is alive,"
And the household forever was numbered at five.
And dumb is the bell that did toll off the hours
And the boys and the blessings, the birds and the flowers,

And dead are the hands that were lifted a space
When the noon seemed to halt while the father said grace!
Here's the place on the jamb where we "reckoned" at night,
There's a mark on the wall where we measured our height,
And a line on the sill where the sunbeam swung round
Like a ship on a bar, as 't was nearing the ground.
Ah, how slowly it crept when some day was to-morrow!
Ah, how swiftly it went I have learned to my sorrow!
Oh, if Gibeon's sun could have shone there of old,
And burnished the sill with unperishing gold!

> The air is alive with a shiver—
>   There's a wandering chill in the room—
> There's a foot that has forded the river—
>   There's a hand feels for mine from a tomb!

I take it in silence, unshrinking,
  And I warm it again in my grasp,
There is nothing of sadness in thinking
  Two worlds may have met in the clasp.
My heart strangely longs as I linger,
  To be decked with some darling old word,
Be clasped as a ring clasps a finger
  By a trinket my boyhood had heard —
Some fragment of speech by love broken,
  As the emblem was broken by Christ,
That, passed round the homestead in token
  Would a soul from a sod have enticed!

Ah, the chimney 'draws' still! It is drawing my heart,
And that rudest of things ever fashioned by art
Does so kindle my soul with intensest desire
To become as a child and see faces in fire,
That I never can wonder the curling blue smoke,
As dull water was wine when Divinity spoke,
Always turned into crimson the instant it broke
Like a glory unrolled into sunshine and air
And then floated abroad like an archangel's hair!
For that chimney was ever the top of the stair

Where *my* Angel came down in the dear Christmas
    Eve ;
Oh, set back the old clock and still let me believe
That the saint of my childhood, Saint Nicholas
    came
Down that tunnel of glory, the route of the flame!
Here the stockings were swung in their red, white,
    and blue,
All fashioned to feet that were light as the dew,
For they walked upon flowers without crushing a
    bud,
That have trampled the flint 'till it blushes with
    blood.
Ah, the fragrant old faith when we watched the
    cold gray
Reluctantly line the dim border of day,
When we braved the bare floor with our little bare
    feet —
No shrine to a pilgrim was ever so sweet.
When each heart and each stocking was burdened
    with bliss —
On the verge of two worlds there is nothing like this
But a mother's last smile and a lover's first kiss !

"Merry Christmas," we cried, and in answer to prayer,
The glad greeting came back like a gush of June air,
That had lurked out the night in those bosoms of theirs
To waylay us at dawn when we stole down the stairs.
God pity the man who has naught to remember,
With no heart anywhere if not in December,
Who abandons the Cross because Romans adore it,
And yet longs for the crown that is carried before it;
Who declaring the birth-day of Christ is uncertain
Would let down on the Manger Oblivion's curtain —
Unheeding the birth of the Heir to the Throne
While he tells off the years, and then honors his own!
Shuts the door on the angels commissioned by Heaven
To belong to the children for one blessed even,
Locks out of their hearts the invisible land,
And tarnishes time with the touch of his hand.

Where the birds had the freedom of window and eaves,
And the walls were all garnished with Bethlehem's sheaves,
The bright straw with its amber bestrewing the floor,
The great eyes of the oxen like lamps at the door,
And their breath clouding up the dim air of the place
As if censers were swinging round altars of grace,
Was the PRINCE of all worlds in humility born,
Who created the Christmas and crowned the new morn.

There were ANGELS without but a flash from the throne,
With the flow of their robes as two mornings in one,
For those angels without brought their glory along,
And they sang to the planet its first Christmas Song.
The Star in the East took its place in the choir,
While the Seraph sang alto the Angels sang air,

And they said: "Unto God all the glory be given!"
Ere it ended on earth it had mounted to heaven —
And they said, and the cadence is lingering still,
" Be His peace evermore to the men of good will!"

There were SHEPHERDS hard by when the carol arose,
And they came as they were, in their every-day clothes;
All above in the blue lay the Lord's shining sheep,
And below in the green were their own fast asleep;
And their hearts of themselves just beginning to sing
What had fluttered to earth like a lark with one wing,
But the anthem's grand surge swept it up to the King!
And that first Christmas Party stood out in the moon
As they watched the transfigured and glorified tune.

And the Magi were seeking the Christmas that day,
And the Star went before them and blazoned the way —

THE CHILD AND THE STAR.

Ah, the children and Christmas together belong,
As the melody marries the words of a song
That can float us right up where the Seraphim
   throng.
With their hands in a tremble the Magi unfold
All their treasures of myrrh and their tokens of gold,
And they swept the brown manger with beards
   like the drift,
As the cloud turns to snow with the moon in the
   rift,
And they led off the world with their first Christ-
   mas Gift.

And the Star and the Manger, the Carol and Child
Have been gladdening the planet since Bethlehem
   smiled.
Bid the singers begin, and the Manger's old chorus
We will sing as *they* sang through the ages before
   us:

  Oh, lift your dull heart from its pillow,
    Let me hold it awhile in my hand,
  Till it warms at the sight of the willow
    As the sailor at sight of the land;

'Till it rallies some soul from its sorrow,
   'Till it smiles the dark winter away,
Lights the hope of a better To - morrow
   With the glow of a brighter To - day.
Let us bid for a cloud to be lifted,
   For a bed that is nothing but straw,
For a hearth that is ashen and drifted
   For a debtor disastered by law;
That the tables of stone may be broken
   And the hearth be an altar of gold,
And the pillow of Bethel betoken
   Not a couch but the Dreamer's of old!
What song was born out of the grieving,
   What a faith in its splendor began,
What worship of God by believing
   In the angel that lingers in man!

Oh, awake in your chambers, ye bells everywhere,
Overturn, oh, ye goblets, and empty in air
All the music that swells to your resonant brims,
'Till ye throb like our hearts, and it blends with our hymns!

Now be thanks to our God that this Eve of the Christmas,
Uniting two worlds with its radiant Isthmus,
And joining again what transgression had riven,
Is the children's own road to the Kingdom of Heaven!
Oh, bells that are iron! Oh, hearts that are human!
Oh, songs that are sweet as the loving of woman!
Be ye blent all the while in a chorus sublime
As the carol of stars by the cradle of Time!
And oh, spare us an angel from Bethlehem's choir,
Let him bring the same song that he helped to sing there,
Be the grand old beatitude sounded again,
And to earth everywhere, Merry Christmas, AMEN!

THANKSGIVING.

LAY out the earth in a sheet of snow,
  There is nothing at all to harm below,
Where men dream out the world together,
And pansies sleep 'till pleasant weather —
The safest place in all the land
Is the narrow realm of the folded hand!
Then THANKS to God that a flower will die,—
'T was made to time Thanksgiving by:
Breathe as it falls — prophetic thing! —
" There 'll be an April in the Spring!"
Then THANKS to God for a sister there
To stand on Glory's diamond stair,
And THANKS again, though I go late,
A mother gone shall smiling wait,
Shall breathe three names with reverent tone,
The Child's, the Virgin's, and her Own,
And lift the latch of Mercy's gate!

II.

Rouse up the fire to a costly glow,
'Till the maple parts and the rubies show!
Swing back the curtains now if ever,
And, rich and warm, the slender river
Shall cleave Thanksgiving-Night in twain
As the mantle parted the old Red Main!—
Ah, never fear—shine as it will,
Enough is left to cheer us still.
Perhaps some wanderer going past,
Who tried all sorrows but the last,
And wonders why he dares to live,
And thinks he has no thanks to give,
May see that glimmer on the ground,—
His old dead heart give glad rebound,—
It looks so like the road of gold
He trod himself in time of old—
Look up and see Thanksgiving found!

III.

Bring out the chairs from the empty wall,
Where fitful shadows used to fall,

The shapes of father, sister, mother,
Of slender sweetheart, friend, and brother.
No painted window half so fair
As the old home-room with its shadows there;
No pictured hall, at king's desire,
Could match that group before the fire,
Who never cast a shade beside,
But on that wall, and when they died!
And some went up at break of day,
Some waited longer by the way;—
Let them who will thank God for light,
Such shadows never made it night.
Come one, come all, there yet is room,
THANKS be to God, from heaven to home
Is nothing but a flash of flight!

IV.

Wheel forth the table, a laden palm,
We'll all give thanks and we'll sing a psalm —
Some song old-fashioned, of Forever,
That floated safe across the river,
No note lost out, no cadence gone,
They warbled, died, and sang right on!

The girls shall come in their white and blue
As if they broke God's azure through,
Played truant to the realms of light
To be with us Thanksgiving night.
The boys are thronging through the hall,
They 've not grown old these years at all!
Some marched away to muffled drum
But fling no shadows as they come —
Without a sorrow or a sin
E'en Death himself would let them in —
Oh, Sweethearts! Comrades! Welcome home!

A POET'S LEGACY.

PAST twenty-one and Love's of age,
   Has lost his wings and gained his eyes,
Looks down on life's unended page,
   Looks up and sees the azure skies.
He's safe to stay while we abide,
   His time for flight forever past,
'T will be we three whate'er betide,
   While roses blow and lilacs last.
No bankrupt Firm is this of ours,
But rich as June in suns and showers.

Bring out the ledger! Every thing
   That men call gains shall be for sale —
Ay, let them go for what they'll bring,
   We'll keep our losses till we fail!

Of old when Judah's children wed,
   They pledged their faith in crimson wine,
Then broke the crystal as they said:
   "No lips shall touch its brim but mine!
"This shall no meaner love profane!"
The shattered symbol fell like rain.

None stooped to pick the fragments up—
   All knew the thing the token meant:
Behold, one love had crowned the cup,
   No matter where the goblet went!
And so, my wife, in Judah's way
   We've drank life's golden draught of wine,
And strown the vase's glittering clay—
   See where the sculptured fragments shine!
The ledger now! Let it be known
How rich and grand this Firm has grown.

The flock of clouds we always keep
   Are marked with rainbows every one,
We know our own celestial sheep
   That throng the blue and graze the sun;
'Tis fine to see them trooping home,
   Their fleeces tangled thick with stars;

'T is fine to watch them as they come
   And wait at Evening's golden bars;
Their shadows fall upon our way,
As if old Night had walked by day

And left her foot-prints as she went;
   Some look like graves of friends that died,
Whose sunken mounds the sward indent,
   Of babe and gallant bridegroom's bride,
Of golden tress and silver hair,—
   And some like hopes our hearts have shed,
That fell as leaves in autumn air
   And crush beneath our thoughtful tread.
Dear wife, we have no clouds to sell,
They make the sunshine *show* so well!

An angel troop this Finn commands,
   A score and one they stand in line,
And swing aloft in radiant hands
   A score and one of Eves divine!
Of Christmas Eves and Christmas bells
   And Christmas gifts with blessing twice
That bring us all, by mystic spells
   In kissing range of Paradise!

My wife, we would not give them up
To mend again the shattered cup!

A score and one of kindling Junes,
   The warm and blushing brides of Time,
Are ranged along like notes in tunes,
   And keep our hearts in rhythmic rhyme.
We own a score of belfryed towers
   Where bird-like wishes bred and born
Are singing songs — those birds are ours —
   We count our twentieth New Year's morn!
No birds to sell, nor songs nor chimes,
We'll keep them all till harder times!

We have some castles gray and grand
   That cloudless suns do shine upon,
Along their halls retainers stand
   And speak Castilian every one.
Nobody dies who dwelleth there,
   They have a clime where tempests swoon,
No graves to make, no empty chair,
   And Christmas in the month of June!
I'll make the deeds — you'll sign them sure,
And castles twelve we'll give the poor!

We've had a wealth of dreams as rife
    As corn along the bladed west,
We have them still in broider'd life
    Like flowers upon a wedding vest.
There comes a little sounder sleep,
    There comes a richer flush of dawn,
'Till then we'll keep our flocks of sheep,
    No castle, cloud, or angel gone.
Down flag of red! We'll make no sale
But hold our losses till we fail!

To make all sure my Will behold:
    "To her who kept this Firm alive
"I now bequeath my clouds of gold,
    "My angel choir, my castles five,
'My score of belfries, all my sheep,
    "The fragments of the sculptured vase,
"To have and hold and ever keep!"
    And yet I've done no act of grace,
They all are yours, but whose are you?
I freely give and keep them too!

THE SONG OF THE AGE.

WOULD ye know the grand song that shall
    sing out the age —
That shall flow down the world as the lines down
    the page —
That shall break through the zones like a North
    and South river,
From winter to spring making music forever?
I heard its first tone by an old-fashioned hearth —
'T was an anthem's faint cry on the brink of its
    birth!
'T was the tea-kettle's drowsy and droning refrain
As it sang through its nose as it swung from the
    crane.

'T was a being begun and awaiting its brains —
To be saddled and bridled and given the reins.

Now its lungs are of steel and its breathings of fire
And it craunches the miles with an iron desire;
Its white cloud of a mane like a banner unfurled,
It howls through the hills and it pants round the world!
It furrows the forest and lashes the flood
And hovers the miles like a partridge's brood!

Oh, stand ye to-day in the door of the heart,
With its nerve raveled out, floating free on the air,
And feeling its way with ethereal art,
By the flash of the telegraph everywhere,
And then think, if you can, of a mission more grand
Than a mission to LIVE in this time and this land,
Round the world for a sweetheart an arm you can wind,
And your lips to the ear of the listening mankind!

JUNE.

THE world is in June and it ripples in rhyme,—
June! Sweetheart of Life and own darling
of Time.
The year, with glad laughter, plays truant to
Death,
Goes back so near Eden she catches its breath,
And follows that airy old fashion of Eve's,
And rustles abroad in an apron of leaves!
She holds her cheek long to the kiss of the sun,
Days widen and warm like some volume begun,
Narrow night like a ribbon just marking the
page
Where some eloquent thought shall last out the
age.
Every bush has a blossom, a bee, or a bird,
A beauty to blow or a hum to be heard —
Battalions of legs — all eyes or all stings —

And billions of monsters, musquitoes, and " things,"
And needles like cherubs, with nothing but wings.
There's a promise to plead or a bill to present,
A grave to be opened, a shroud to be rent,
For they rise without trump; resurrections in
    June
Are as blithe as the lark and as bonny as Doon.
From the tick of a heart in the breast of a wren
To the trumpets that make Agamemnons of men,—
From the tear drop that trembles unflashed from
    its brim
To the surly old storm that rolls over earth's rim,
Tramples out the white stars as daisies are trod,
While its red plumage shakes with the drum-beat
    of God,
Till green world and blue world by tempest are
    riven
And the lightnings' dread squadrons charge right
    up to Heaven,
As Sheridan went—as if grim Mission Ridge
With its arches of fire were the pier of a bridge
Somebody had built to the gates of the sky
And he bound to go up without waiting to die—

Everything, everywhere, struggling up in the strife,
Is beginning to climb that strange ladder of life,
With an angel alight on its uppermost round
And an atom alive where it touches the ground.
From the blue music-box of the robin's old wife
A burglar breaks through into mansions of life.

Hearts are trumps here in June : heart of lion and
    lark,
Heart of Richard and Rachel and Joan of Arc ;
Heart of iron and oak, steady, sturdy, and true,
When through lines of red fire broke the jackets
    of blue ;
A world of life's rivers all ebbing and flowing,
A world full of hearts like hammers all going,
Yet instead of our *hearing* these drummers of
    wonder
With their ruffle and roll pulsing out into thunder,
The earth is, for all of this turbulent crowd,
As still as a star, or the shape in a shroud.

I think it was June when the maiden looked down
On the dear little Moses just ready to drown,

And, his basket of bulrushes rocked by the Nile,
That Columbus of Canaan looked up with a smile!

When summer's green surges roll over the land
Till you hardly can tell as they break on the strand,
Where this world doth end or the other begin,
They so hide all the graves, the first footprints of sin,
Is it strange that Earth's singers should drift out of June,
As if lifted by chance on the swell of a tune,
And fairly float over life's musical bars,
When the birds can go with them half way to the stars?
So went Sontag and Weber — magnificent pair! —
He was clerk to the angels and she sang in the choir;
He recorded in score, but she passed down the word
Till a turbulent world grew human and heard.
Ah, talk of the eye unsleeping, unweeping,
Undaunted, undying, its watch and ward keeping,

To whose glance telescopic raveled midnight is
  given —
You can see to Orion, but you *hear* into Heaven!

So went they in June who with wonderful art
Put in English and rhythm the beat of the heart —
The bard of Sweet Hope and the bard of Sweet
  Home.
They wronged thee, oh Sexton! They tenant no
  tomb,
For Campbell shall live when the tartan is dim,
And Payne walk the world that is chanting his
  hymn.

How came they in June who the rainbow unbent
And laid it alive on the fold of a tent;
With fingers immortal the curtain withdrew
And the canvas was kindled and faces looked
  through —
Lips ruddy and ripe with the old loving glow
Somebody was kissing three ages ago!
So Rubens, June born, the grand master of art,
With a nerve in his pencil strung straight from his
  heart,

At whose touch the Evangels gave Calvary up,
The Christ and the Cross and the Crown and the Cup—
And Hebrew and Greek fell away from the story
And left it sublime in its gloom and its glory!

And that Spaniard, June born, whose fame shed a gleam
Ere Plymouth had pilgrim or Bunyan a dream—
With no drop of blue blood in breast or in brain,
By a right far diviner than Philip's of Spain,
Was own king of colors—whose banners so brave
Never lowered unto death, never struck to the grave;
Pride and pomp of the realm the Armada went down,
Cleared the face of the sea like a vanishing frown,
But some child that he painted, its journey undone,
Makes the transit of ages as Venus the sun!

Christ lay in thy manger, oh, fairest of stars!
June rocks in thy cradle, oh, brighter than Mars—

God walked in thy garden — man sprung from thy
   dust —
Ah, who would not hold thy grand story in trust,
That no blade would be wielded nor battle be
   born,
But the green waving sabres by ranks of young
   corn?
Yet what broods of grim thunders have nested in
   June,
Swooped from eyries of blue in the broad summer
   noon,
Splashed the greenest sod red with the color of
   fame,
Flared the flags into flower with their breathings
   of flame,
And growled the world dumb — all its eloquent
   words,
The laugh of its girls and the songs of its birds.
Marengo roars down the long highway sublime,
'Tis the Corsican clocks striking Bonaparte's
   time —
The grumble of guns that had hidden the stars
From the sands of the Nile to the land of the Czars;

Old Monmouth breaks in with its rattle and rain
To the flash of the flint and "mad Anthony
    Wayne."

And Cromwell the trooper, half lamb and half lion,
For the wicked King Charles and the blessèd
    Mount Zion—
Two hundred years nearer Time's morning than
    now,
Rode into the storm naked blade and bare brow,
Wheeled his surly old squadrons as the Lord wheels
    a cloud—
Their hearts and their cannon all throbbing aloud—
And rode down the King with a cavalry shock
That smote off his crown, bent his head to the
    block,
Made royalists tremble and monarchy rock!

But the throb of no battery ever has stirred
The world's mighty heart like some stout English
    word,
Wherein a brave utterance sandaled and shod
Has marched down the ages for Freedom and God!

JUNE.

'Mid the splendor of June the roar of the Shannon
Roused something more grand than the Chesa-
    peake's cannon,
For she wrung out the words from Lawrence's lip
That shall linger for ever: "Do n't give up the
    ship!"
Ah, the click of flint locks is not half so divine
As the click of the type as they fall into line,
The audible step of unfaltering feet
To a mightier tune than our bosoms can beat.

I remember the heroes who sailed out of June,
Ross, Harvey, and Franklin, and Hudson's "Half
    Moon,"
Into realms where the sea has breathlessly stood
Like the scalps of the Alps dumb and white before
    God;
Who have bended the oar and have lifted the
    wing,
Fairly fled the dominions of caliph and king,
Broken out of horizons as old as mankind,
Shatter'd shells of the worlds they were leaving
    behind.

Aye, Harvey, who stood by the brink of a heart,
And saw it brim over, turn crimson and start,
And discovered a river as truly God's own
As the river of crystal that flows by His throne.

Bear away, ye tall ships, farewell and all hail!
Cloud up, main and mizzen, weigh anchor, and sail!
Be lifted blue Heaven! Let the admirals through,
There's a lubber ashore that is grander than you!
Born of rags and flung down on a marvelous street,
All rough with the prints of a million of feet,
And cradled in iron and trampled with ink,
This poor dingy creature, I venture to think,
The frailest and feeblest of fluttering things,
As easily crushed as a butterfly's wings,
Has more power, oh, ye ships, than your canvas of white
To let out the world and to let in the light,
And swing from their hinges the portals of night.

Let the ashes of Smithfield tell, if they can,
When this gift of the Pentecost fell upon man.

It was born out of doors in that faded old June
When the chime of Christ's ages struck twelve
    o'clock noon,
And the barons of John plucked the heart of this
    thing,
The Charter of Liberty, warm from the King.

Imperial June of the emerald crown!
When angels had read the Lord's weather-roll
    down,
They found but one June in all Heaven to spare,
And direct by the route of the answer to prayer
From the glory above thou didst fall through the
    air.

OCTOBER.

I.

I WOULD not die in May:
   When orchards drift with blooms of white like
      billows on the deep,
And whispers from the Lilac bush across my senses
      sweep,
That 'mind me of a girl I knew when life was
      always May,
Who filled my nights with starry hopes that faded
      out by day —
When time is full of wedding-days, and nests of
      robins brim,
'Till overflows their wicker sides the old familiar
      hymn —
The window brightens like an eye, the cottage
      doors swing wide.
The boys come homeward one by one and bring a
      smiling bride,

The fire-fly shows her signal light, the partridge
    beats his drum,
And all the world gives promise of something
    sweet to come —
        Ah, who would die on such a day?
        Ah, who would die in May?

II.

    I would not die in June:
When looking up with faces quaint the pansies
    grace the sod,
And looking down, the willows see their doubles
    in the flood —
When blessing God we breathe again the roses in
    the air,
And lilies light the fields along with their immortal wear
As once they lit the Sermon of the Saviour on the
    Mount,
And glorified the story they evermore recount —
Through pastures blue the flocks of God go trooping one by one,
And turn their golden fleeces round to dry them
    in the sun —

When calm as Galilee the grain is rippling in the
  wind,
And nothing dying anywhere but something that
  has sinned —
        Ah, who would die in life's own noon?
        Ah, who would die in June?

III.

    But when OCTOBER comes,
And poplars drift their leafage down in flakes of
  gold below,
And beeches burn like twilight fires that used to
  tell of snow,
And maples bursting into flame set all the hills
  a-fire,
And Summer from her evergreens sees Paradise
  draw nigher —
A thousand sunsets all at once distil like Hermon's
  dew,
And linger on the waiting woods and stain them
  through and through,
As if all earth had blossomed out, one grand Co-
  rinthian flower,
To crown Time's graceful capital for just one
  gorgeous hour!

They strike their colors to the king of all the
    stately throng —
He comes in pomp, OCTOBER! To him all times
    belong:
The frost is on his sandals but the flush is on his
    cheeks,
September sheaves are in his arms, June voices
    when he speaks —
The elms lift bravely like a torch within a Grecian
    hand,
See where they light the Monarch on through all
    the splendid land!
The sun puts on a human look behind the hazy
    fold,
The mid-year moon of silver is struck anew in
    gold,
In honor of the very day that Moses saw of old,
For in the Burning Bush that blazed as quenchless
    as a sword
The old Lieutenant first beheld OCTOBER and the
    LORD!
        Ah, then, October, let it be —
        I'll claim my dying day from thee!

TORNADO SUNDAY.

THE winds sweetly sung
  In the elms as they swung,
And the woods were in time and the robins in tune;
  One cloud just forgiven,
  Lay at anchor in heaven.
And Iowa asleep on the threshold of June!

  All the air a great calm,
  And the prairie a palm,
For the Lord when He blest, left the print of His
    hand —
  All the roses in blow,
  All the rivers a-glow,
Thus the Sabbath came down on the bud-laden
    land.

  On the bride and the bold,
  On the clay and the gold,

On the furrow unfinish 'd, on fame to be won,
    On the turbulent tide,
    On the river's green side
Where the flocks of white villages lay in the sun.

    All the world was in rhyme —
    Bid good morning to Time!
Oh, sweet bells and sweet words of the dear golden
    Then!
    It is fair all abroad
    From blue sky to green sod!
Let us pray while we can: blessèd Sabbath, Amen!

    Not a murmur in air,
    Nor lament anywhere,
And no footfall of God on the ledges of cloud;
    'T was a breath, and it fled —
    Song and Sabbath were dead,
And the threads of gold sunshine the woof of the
    shroud.

    Oh, words never spoken,
    Oh, heart and hearth broken,

Oh, beautiful paths such as loving feet wear!
    All erased from the land,
    Like a name in the sand —
As the thistle-down drifts on a billow of air!

    Like the sighing of leaves
    When the winter wind grieves,
Like the rattle of chariots driving afar,
    Like the wailing of woods,
    Like the rushing of floods,
Like the clang of huge hammers a-forging a star!

    Like a shriek of despair
    In the shivering air,
Like the rustle of banners with tempest abroad,
    Like a soul out of heaven,
    Like a tomb trumpet-riven,
Like a syllable dropp'd from the thunder of God!

    Then these to their weeping,
    And those to their sleeping,
And the blue wing of heaven was over them all!
    Oh "sweet south" that singeth,
    Oh, flower girl that bringeth
The gushes of fragrance to hovel and hall!

Oh, blue-bird, shed Spring
With the flash of thy wing,
Where December drifts cold in the bosom of June—
Set our hearts to the words,
Dear as songs of first birds:
We are Brothers at night that were strangers at noon!

THE SKYLARK.

I HELD in my hand a wonder — a hymn of a
    thousand years;
It was born in an English meadow — it was older
    than English cheers —
'Twas a hymn for the Roman eagles and a psalm
    for the Norman Line —
It was sung through the wars of the Roses, when
    the York turned red as wine —
It was heard on Bosworth field, when Gloster's
    flint struck fire,
And Richard's soul to Richmond's steel did glim-
    mer and expire;
When the peans for the thane drowned the dirges
    for the thing,
And *he* swept across the planet on fame's eternal
    wing,
Who waged the battle as an earl but won it as a
    king,

And plucked the crown of England from the hawthorn where it hung,
And lightly to his longing brow Golconda's cluster swung,
The crown upon the coronet, till the light of its pearls grew thin
And pale as a morning star that has led the daylight in.

Charge! and Marston Moor was a drum by galloping cavalry beat,
Halt! and each iron rank brought up with a clank, and each trooper sat still in his seat.
Hark! and down from the blue to the red was floating that exquisite strain,
As if every rider had ridden, and never drawn sabre or rein,
Right out of the hell of the battle to the door of heaven ajar,
And thought he heard before his time the singing of a star,
And thought he saw in the downy cloud the truant from the choir,
As it hung in sweet libration — an anthem in the air.

And I held in my hand that wonder — a book with a single psalm,
That would not brim the hollow of a woman's loving palm;
And the lyric was brown breasted, and the lids of the book were wings,
And the bird was an English skylark, and the feeblest of God's things.
That had fallen out of the azure like a mote from a mighty eye.
And had shared the fate of the sparrow, for the Father saw him die.
Oh, bravest bird of Britain! — a little ounce of death —
Oh, song born out of heaven! — a clod without a breath.

And then my soul grew reverent — my heart beat strong and grand.
As I thought of the broad commission of the atom in my hand;
That the Admiral of the fleets at anchor off the world,
Flung out his pennant with a touch that little pinion furled —

Unrolled the scrolls of thunder, 'twixt the seraph and the sod,
Dashed down a word of fire in the running hand of God,
And stamped the stormy margins with His ring so broad and brave,
One half is in the welkin — the other in the wave:
By Him to meet that bird mid-air, the misty morn was driven,
Lest it should break away from earth and sing itself to heaven;
He sowed the Grand Armada like grain upon the breeze,
But gave to lark and lightning the freedom of the seas!

The cattle asleep in the meadow and the shadows asleep on the hill,
And the mists, like gray Franciscans, all standing ghostly still —
And the stars are drowsily shutting their eyes as weary watchers will —

And the crescent moon in the west shows the flash of a silver shoe,
As the steed that brought over the midnight is bearing it down the blue,
And out of the silence and shadow there quivered the slenderest song,
And a bird going up in the morning exultantly followed along —
And the mountains stood down in their places and the clouds all timidly clung,
But a strand of Jehovah untwisted whereon the lost Pleiads are strung,
When this bird with its music and motion, ere the dawn had blooded its breast,
Up direct from the sod to the glory of God, triumphantly burst from the nest.

BUNKER HILL.

TO the wail of the fife and the snarl of the drum
   Those Hedgers and Ditchers of Bunker Hill come,
Down out of the battle with rumble and roll,
Straight across the two ages, right into the soul,
And bringing for captive the Day that they won
With a deed that like Joshua halted the sun.
Like bells in their towers tolled the guns from the town,
Beat that low earthen bulwark so sullen and brown,
As if Titans last night had plowed the one bout
And abandoned the field for a Yankee redoubt;
But for token of life that the parapet gave
They might as well play on Miles Standish's grave!
Then up the green hill rolled the red of the Georges
And down the green vale rolled the grime of the forges —

Ten rods from the ridges hung the live surge,
Not a murmur to meet it broke over the verge,
But the click of flint-locks in the furrows along,
And the chirp of a sparrow just singing her song.
In the flash of an eye, as the dead shall be raised,
The dull bastion kindled, the parapet blazed,
And the musketry cracked, glowing hotter and higher,
Like a forest of hemlock, its lashes of fire.
And redder the scarlet and riven the ranks,
And Putnam's guns hung, with a roar on the flanks.
Now the battle grows dumb and the grenadiers wheel,
'Tis the crash of clubbed musket, the thrust of cold steel,
At bay all the way, while the guns held their breath,
Foot to foot, eye to eye, with each other and Death.
Call the roll, Sergeant Time! Match the day if you can:
Waterloo was for Britons—Bunker Hill is for man!

THE OLD VILLAGE CHOIR.

I HAVE fancied sometimes the Bethel-bent beam
   That trembled to earth in the Patriarch's dream,
Was a ladder of song in that wilderness rest
From the pillow of stone to the blue of the Blest,
And the angels descending to dwell with us here,
" Old Hundred " and " Corinth " and " China " and " Mear."

All the hearts are not dead nor under the sod
That those breaths can blow open to Heaven and God.
Ah, " Silver Street " flows by a bright shining road,—
Oh, not to the *hymns* that in harmony flowed,
But the sweet human psalms of the old-fashioned choir,
To the girl that sang alto, the girl that sang air.

"Let us sing to God's praise!" the minister said:
All the psalm-books at once fluttered open at
    "York,"
Sunned their long dotted wings in the words that
    he read,
While the leader leaped into the tune just ahead,
And politely picked up the key-note with a fork,
And the vicious old viol went growling along
At the heels of the girls in the rear of the song.

Oh, I need not a wing;—bid no genii come
With a wonderful web from Arabian loom,
To bear me again up the river of Time,
When the world was in rhythm and life was its
    rhyme,
And the stream of the years flowed so noiseless
    and narrow
That across it there floated the song of a sparrow;
For a sprig of green caraway carries me there,
To the old village church and the old village choir,
Where clear of the floor my feet slowly swung
And timed the sweet pulse of the praise that they
    sung,

Till the glory aslant from the afternoon sun
Seemed the rafters of gold in God's temple begun!

You may smile at the nasals of old Deacon Brown
Who followed by scent till he ran the tune down,
And dear sister Green, with more goodness than grace,
Rose and fell on the tunes as she stood in her place,
And where "Coronation" exultantly flows,
Tried to reach the high notes on the tips of her toes!
To the land of the leal they have gone with their song,
Where the choir and the chorus together belong.
Oh! be lifted, ye gates! Let me hear them again,
Blessèd song! Blessèd Singers! forever, Amen.

GOING HOME.

DRAWN by horses with decorous feet,
    A carriage for one went through the street:
Polished as anthracite out of the mine,
Tossing its plumes so stately and fine,
As nods to the night a Norway pine.

The passenger lay in Parian rest,
As if, by the Sculptor's hand caressed,
A mortal life through the marble stole,
And then till an Angel calls the roll
It waits awhile for a human soul.

He rode in state, but his carriage-fare
Was left unpaid to his only heir;
Hardly a man from hovel to throne
Takes to this route in coach of his own,
But borrows at last and travels alone.

GOING HOME.

The driver sat in his silent seat,
The world as still as a field of wheat
Gave all the road to the speechless twain,
And thought the passenger never again
Should travel that way with living men.

Not a robin held its little breath,
But sang right on in the face of death;
You never would dream to see the sky
Give glance for glance to the violet's eye,
That aught between them ever could die.

A wain bound East met the hearse bound **West**,
Halted a moment, and passed abreast;
And I verily think a stranger pair
Have never met on a thoroughfare,
Or a dim by-road, or anywhere:

The hearse as slim and glossy and still
As silken thread at a woman's will,
Who watches her work with tears unshed,
Broiders a grief with needle and thread,
Mourns in pansies and cypress the dead;

Spotless the steeds in a satin dress,
That run for two worlds, the Lord's Express —
Long as the route of Arcturus's ray,
Brief as the Publican's trying to pray,
No other steeds by no other way
Could go so far in a single day.

From wagon broad and heavy and rude
A group looking out from a single hood:
Striped with the flirt of a heedless lash,
Dappled and dimmed with many a splash,
" Gathered " behind like an old calash,

It made you think of a schooner's sail
Mildewed with weather, tattered by gale,
Down " by the run " from mizzen and main —
That canvas mapped with stipple and stain
Of Western earth and the prairie rain.

The watch-dog walked in his ribs between
The hinder wheels with sleepy mien;
A dangling pail to the axle slung;
Astern of the wain a manger hung —
A schooner's boat by the davits swung.

The white-faced boys sat three in a row,
With eyes of wonder and heads of tow;
Father looked sadly over his brood:
Mother just lifted a flap of the hood;
All saw the hearse — and *two* understood.

They thought of the one-eyed cabin small,
Hid like a nest in the grasses tall,
Where plains swept boldly off in the air,
Grooved into heaven everywhere —
So near the stars' invisible stair

That planets and prairie almost met —
Just cleared its edges as they set!
They thought of the level world's "divide,"
And their hearts flowed down its other side
To the little grave of the girl that died.

They thought of childhood's neighborly hills
With sunshine aprons and ribbons of rills,
That drew so near when the day went down,
Put on a crimson and golden crown
And sat together in mantles brown;

The dawn's red plume in their winter caps,
And Night asleep in their drowsy laps,
Light 'ning the load of the shouldered wood
By shedding the shadows as they could,
That gathered round where the homestead stood.

They thought — that pair in the rugged wain,
Thinking with bosom rather than brain;
They 'll never know till their dying day
That what they thought and never could say,
Their hearts throbbed out in an Alpine lay,
The old Waldensian song again:
Thank God for the mountains, and Amen!

The wain gave a lurch, the hearse moved on —
A moment or two, and both were gone;
The wain bound East, the hearse bound West,
Both going home, both looking for rest,—
The Lord save all, and His name be blest!

THE DEAD GRENADIER.

ON the right of the battalion a grenadier of France,
Struck through his iron harness by the lightning of a lance,
His breast all wet with British blood, his brow with British breath,
There fell defiant, face to face with England and with death.
They made a mitre of his heart — they cleft it through and through —
One half was for his legion, and the other for it too!
The colors of a later day prophetic fingers shed,
For lips were blue and cheeks were white and the *fleur de lis* was red!
And the bugles blew, and the legion wheeled, and the grenadier was dead.

And then the old commander rode slowly down
    the ranks,
And thought how *brief* the journey grew, between
    the battered flanks;
And the shadows in the moonlight fell strangely
    into line
Where the battle's reddest riot pledged the richest
    of the wine,
And the camp-fires flung their phantoms—all
    doing what they could
To close the flinty columns up as old campaigners
    would!
On he rode, the old commander, with the ensign
    in advance,
And, as statued bronzes brighten with the smoky
    torch's glance,
Flashed a light in all their faces, like the flashing
    of a lance,
When, with brow all bare and solemn, "For the
    King!" he grandly said,
"Lower the colors to the living—beat the ruffle
    for the dead!"

And thrice the red silk flickered low its flame of
  royal fire,
And thrice the drums moaned out aloud the
  mourner's wild desire.
Ay, lower again thou crimson cloud—again ye
  drums lament—
'Tis Rachel in the wilderness and Ramah in the
  tent!

"Close up! Right dress!" the Captain said, and
  they gathered under the moon,
As the shadows glide together when the sun shines
  down at noon—
A stranger at each soldier's right—ah, war's wild
  work is grim!—
And so to the last of the broken line, and Death at
  the right of him!
And there, in the silence deep and dead, the Sergeant called the roll,
And the name went wandering down the lines as
  he called a passing soul.
Oh, then that a friendly mountain that summons
  might have heard,

And flung across the desert dumb the shadow of
  the word,
And caught the name that all forlorn along the
  legion ran,
And clasped it to its mighty heart and sent it back
  to man!

There it stood, the battered legion, while the Sergeant called the roll,
And the name went wandering down the lines as
  he called for a passing soul.
Hurrah for the dumb, dead lion! And a voice for
  the grenadier
Rolled out of the ranks like a drum-beat, and
  sturdily answered "HERE!"
"He stood," cried the sons of thunder, and their
  hearts ran over the brim,
"He stood by the old battalion, and we'll always
  stand by him!
"Ay, call for the grand crusader, and we'll answer
  to the name."
"And what will ye say?" the Sergeant said.
  "DEAD ON THE FIELD OF FAME!"

And dare ye call that dying? The dignity sublime
That gains a furlough from the grave, and then reports to Time?
Doth earth give up the daisies to a little sun and rain,
And keep at their roots the heroes while weary ages wane?

Sling up the trumpet, Israfeel! Sweet bugler of our God,
For nothing waits thy summons beneath this broken sod;
They march abreast with the ages to the thunder on the right,
For they bade the world " GOOD MORNING " when the world had said " GOOD NIGHT!"

RHYMES OF THE RIVER.

OH River far-flowing,
    How broad thou art growing!
And the sentinel head-lands wait grimly for thee;
    And Euroclydon urges
    The bold-riding surges,
That in white-crested lines gallop in from the sea

    O bright-hearted river,
    With crystalline quiver,
Like a sword from its scabbard, far-flashing
    abroad!
    And I think, as I gaze
    On the tremulous blaze,
That thou surely wert drawn by an angel of God!

    Through the black-heart of night,
    Leaping out to the light,

Thou art reeking with sunset and dyed with the
    dawn ;
    Cleft the emerald sod —
    Cleft the mountains of God —
And the shadows of roses yet rusted thereon !

    Where willows are weeping,
    Where shadows are sleeping,
Where the frown of the mountain lies dark on thy
    crest ;
    Arcturus now shining,
    Arbutus now twining,
And " my castles in Spain " gleaming down in thy
    breast ;

    Then disastered and dim,
    Swinging sullen and grim,
Where the old ragged shadows of hovels are
    shed ;
    Creeping in, creeping out,
    As in dream, or in doubt,
In the reeds and the rushes slow rocking the
    dead.

When all crimson and gold,
Slowly home to the fold
Do the fleecy clouds flock to the gateway of even,
Then, no longer brook-born,
But a way paved with morn,
Ay, a bright golden street to the city of Heaven!

In the great stony heart
Of the feverish mart,
Is the throb of thy pulses pellucid, to-day;
By gray mossy ledges,
By green velvet edges,
Where the corn waves its sabre, thou glidest away.

Broad and brave, deep and strong,
Thou art lapsing along;
And the stars rise and fall in thy turbulent tide,
As light as the drifted
White swan's breast is lifted,
Or a June fleet of lilies at anchor may ride.

And yet, gallant river,
On-flashing forever,
That hast cleft the broad world on thy way to the
    main,
I would part from thee here,
With a smile and a tear,
And a Hebrew, read back to thy fountains again.

Ah, well I remember,
Ere dying December
Would fall like a snow-flake and melt on thy
    breast,
O'er thy waters so narrow
The little brown sparrow
Used to send his low song to his mate on the nest.

With a silvery skein
Wove of snow and of rain,
Thou didst wander at will through the bud-laden
    land,—
All the air a sweet psalm,
And the meadow a palm,—
As a blue vein meanders a liberal hand.

When the school-master's daughter
With her hands scooped the water,
And laughingly proffered the crystal to me,
Oh, there ne'er sparkled up
A more exquisite cup
Than the pair of white hands that were brimming
with thee!

And there all together,
In bright summer weather,
Did we loiter with thee along thy green brink;
And how silent we grew
If the robin came too,
When he looked up to pray, and then bent down
to drink!

Ah, where are the faces,
From out thy still places,
That so often smiled back in those soft days of
May?
As we bent hand in hand,
Thou didst double the band,
As idle as daisies — and fleeting as they!

Like the dawn in the cloud
Lay the babe in its shroud,
And a rose-bud was clasped in its frozen white
    hand : —
At the mother's last look
It had opened the book,
As if sweet-breathing June were abroad in the
    land !

O pure placid river
Make music forever
In the gardens of Paradise, hard by the throne !
For on thy far shore,
Gently drifted before,
We may find the lost blossoms that once were our
    own.

Ah, beautiful river,
Flow onward forever !
Thou art grander than Avon, and sweeter than Ayr ;
If a tree has been shaken,
If a star has been taken,
In thy bosom we look — bud and Pleiad are there !

    I take up the old words,
    Like the song of dead birds,
That were breathed when I stood farther off from
        the sea:
    When I heard not its hymn,
    When the headlands were dim:—
Shall I ever again weave a rhythm for thee?

LAZY.

UNDER the maple tree lying supine,
    Timing the beat of a pendulum vine,
Swinging the Delawares turning to wine.

Gazing straight upward a mile in the blue,
Watching a cloud that has nothing to do,
Wishing a deed for an acre or two;

Nothing to do but come down in the rain,
Born of the mist unto Heaven again,
Nothing to sow and no reaping of grain.

Watching a bee in his pollen pant'loon
Droning him home in the chrysolite noon,
Ghost of a drummer-boy drumming a tune.

Watching a jay on the cherry tree nigh,
Stranger to love, with its cruel bright eye;
What of that jacket as blue as the sky?

Splashing his crest with the cherry's red blood,
Jauntiest robber that ranges the wood,
Nothing will name him but blue Robin Hood.

Hearing a bird with her English all right
Calling somebody from morning till night,
Waiting forever the mystic " Bob White."

Woman's own cousin since Adam began,
Beautiful Voice that is wanting a man,
Quail in a coif of the time of Queen Anne.

Counting the leaves as they drift from the rose
Strowing with fragrance my place of repose;
Dying?   Ah no, only changing its clothes.

Watching a spider pay out her last line,
Working at Euclid's Geometry fine,
Web is all woven and weaver will dine!

Watching a fly laze along to its doom,
Silken the meshes but death in the loom,
Shrouded and eaten but never a tomb!

Sparrow a-drowse on a limb overhead,
Opens an eye when the spider is fed,
Opens a bill and the spider is dead!

Watching a butterfly slowly unfold,
Crowning a post with a blossom of gold
Strange as the rod that did blossom of old.

Hinged on a life is the duplicate page,
Lettered in light by a wiser than sage,
Lasting a summer and read for an age.

Burst from the bonds! For that coffin was *thine*,
Tenantless thing where the sycamores shine,
Riven and rent and the worm is divine!

Born from the dust and its veriest slave,
Hail to the herald direct from the grave!
Pinion of beauty, resplendently wave!

Bringing from far, what no angel could say,
Something of them who have vanished away,
Left me alone on this amethyst day.

Rent is the chrysalis hid in the sod,
All the dear tenantry dwelling abroad,
Gone through the gate of the glory of God!

DEARBORN OBSERVATORY.

FROM my chamber last night I looked out on the sky
No mortal can reach without waiting to die,
And I saw a few ships of Infinity's fleet,
And the light at their bows lit the dew in the street
That dying men crush with irreverent feet.
Broadside to this port ridged and roughened with graves,
Not a boat from the shore, not a gun from the waves,
There they lay off and on in the Blue of the Blest
Like the thoughts of the Lord in His sabbath-day rest!
Are we chained here for life? Are we bound to the clod
When the lark with a song springs direct from the sod
To the breakers of day and the glory of God?

Have you heard of the man who was calling the roll
Of the stars till the Seraphim called for his soul?
Who began the Lord's census and prayed for clear
    night
While he counted for life the squadrons of light?
Do you know how the Pleiads made sail at the
    word
And Arcturus bore down, till he fancied he heard
The wash of the sky as it rocked off a shore
It never had touched at a signal before!
Port of Entry for stars! Where great admirals
    come
And flotillas report to a Herschel at home —
In that wonderful tower whose window commands
Not a thing in the universe fashioned with hands.
There's an eye at the window that never can sleep,
That no ages can dim and that never can weep —
Always gazing at life, never seeing the graves,
Though the land with its tombs mocks the sea with
    its waves —
That beckons a world and it dawns into sight,
Gives a glance at the blue and it sparkles with
    light.

H

Sweeps a field that the Lord had forgotten to sow
When He scattered the worlds like His treasures
    of snow,
And a sun blossoms out of the infinite space
Like the first flower of Spring in God's garden of
    grace.
Oh, second Fort Dearborn! Oh, Lookout sublime!
Stand fast till God's morning shall break upon time!

JENNIE JUNE.

LIKE a foundling in slumber, the summer day lay
   On the crimsoning threshold of even,
And I thought that the glow through the azure-arched way
   Was a glimpse of the coming of Heaven.
There together we sat by the beautiful stream,
We had nothing to do but to love and to dream
   In the days that have gone on before,
These are not the same days, though they bear the same name,
   With the ones I shall welcome no more.

But it may be that angels are culling them o'er
   For a Sabbath and summer forever;
When the years shall forget the Decembers they wore,
   And the shroud shall be woven, no, never.

In a twilight like that, Jennie June for a bride,
Oh! what more of the world could one wish for beside,
   As we gazed on the river unrolled,
Till we heard, or we fancied, its musical tide
   When it flowed through the gateway of gold!

"Jennie June," then I said, "let us linger no more
   "On the banks of the beautiful river;
"Let the boat be unmoored, and be muffled the oar,
   "And we'll steal into heaven together.
"If the angel on duty our coming descries,
"You have nothing to do but throw off the disguise
   "That you wore while you wandered with me,
"And the sentry shall say, 'Welcome back to the skies,
   "'We long have been waiting for thee.'"

Oh, how sweetly she spoke, ere she uttered a word,
   With that blush, partly hers, partly even's;
And a tone like the dream of a song we once heard,
   As she whispered, "This way is not heaven's,

"For the river that runs by the realm of the blest
"Has no song on its ripple, no star on its breast:
    "Oh! *that* river is nothing like this:
"For it glides on in shadow, beyond the world's West,
    "Till it breaks into beauty and bliss."

I am lingering yet, but I linger alone,
    On the banks of the beautiful river:
'T is the twin of that day, but the wave where it shone
    Bears the willow-tree's shadow for ever.

BURNS' CENTURY SONG.

I.

HOPE, her starry vigil keeping
   O'er a Campbell by the Clyde —
By the Tweed a " Wizard " sleeping —
   " Shepherd " by the Yarrow's side —
Land of glory, song, and story,
Land of mountains and of men,
   Did ye dream that Song could die?
Banks and braes be glad again,
   ROBERT BURNS is passing by!

   Everywhere, everywhere,
Smiles will break and tears will start,
Making rainbows round the heart,
   Ploughman, Brother, BARD OF AYR!

II.

Heart of leal! Can this be dying,
    Coming thus sublimely down!
Lo, an hundred winters sighing
    Leave unstrown thy holly crown!
Not in sorrow dawns thy morrow,
" Bonny Jean" is by thy side,
    Making life and love keep time;
Beauty be thy deathless bride,
    Weaving all our hearts in rhyme!

III.

Heavy heart and smoky rafter
    Growing light with Burns's song —
Calmer tears and clearer laughter —
    Plaided bosoms brave and strong;
Birds are singing, blue-bells ringing,
Naked Heart in open palm!
    With thy " days of auld lang syne,"
With thy Cotter's evening Psalm,
    Thou hast made all ages thine.

IV.

Now the thrush's silver sonnet
    Trembling from the blossom'd thorn,
Winter floating white upon it—
    Sweetest Lyric ever born!
BRUCE is breaking—WALLACE waking,
From the clasp of mighty Death,
    Morven swells the Doric song!—
Lads' and lassies' blended breath,
    Gushes sweet all summer long!

V.

O'er the daisy in the furrow
    Bending low with loving words—
By the mouse's broken burrow—
    Songs of burnies and of birds—
Breezes blowing—rivers flowing—
Hark, the beat of bonny DOON,
    LOGAN, DEVON, AFTON, AYR,
Braided in a pleasant tune,
    "HIGHLAND MARY" in the choir!

Everywhere, everywhere,
Smiles will break and tears will start,
Making rainbows round the heart,
Ploughman, Brother, BARD OF AYR!

THE COLORED MARBLE.

ON marble beds where violets die
   And the moss rose pillows its pride,
The marble looks like an azure sky
   Where a cloudless day has died.

The years go by, and out of the shroud
   The statue stands naked in noon;
Out of the tint and out of the cloud
   Of a long-forgotten June!

*FLOWER*S.

FLOWERS bloom in Christ's Sermon, and all
the year long
You can gather a " Sharon " from Solomon's Song.

THE NEW CRAFT IN THE OFFING.

'TWAS a beautiful night on a beautiful deep,
And the man at the helm had just fallen asleep,
And the watch on the deck, with his head on his breast,
Was beginning to dream that another's it pressed,
When the look-out aloft cried, "A sail! ho! a sail!"
And the question and answer went rattling like hail:
"A sail! ho! a sail!" "Where away?" "No'th-no'th-West!"
"Make her out?" "No, your honor." The din drowned the rest.

There indeed is the stranger, the first in these seas,
Yet she drives boldly on in the teeth of the breeze.

Now her bows to the breakers she steadily turns,
Oh! how brightly the light of her binnacle burns!
Not a signal for Saturn this rover has given,
No salute for our Venus, the flag-star of heaven;
Not a rag or a ribbon adorning her spars,
She has saucily sailed by " the red planet Mars;"
She has doubled triumphant the cape of the Sun
And the sentinel stars, without firing a gun!
" Helm a-port!" " Show a light!" " She will run us aground!"
" Fire a gun!" " Bring her to!" " Sail a-hoy!"
" Whither bound?"

Avast there, ye lubbers! Leave the rudder alone:
'T is a craft in commission — the Admiral's own;
And she sails with sealed orders, unopened as yet,
Though her anchors she weighed before Lucifer set.
Ah, she sails by a chart no draughtsman could make,
Where each cloud that can trail and each wave that can break;

Where that sparkling flotilla, the Asteroids, lie,
Where the scarf of red Morning is flung on the sky;
Where the breath of the sparrow is staining the air —
On the chart that she bears you will find them all there!
Let her pass on in peace to the port whence she came,
With her trackings of fire and her streamers of flame!

THE VANE ON THE SPIRE.

THERE'S an arrow aloft with a feather'd shaft
  That never has flown at the bow-string's draft,
And the goldsmith has hidden the blacksmith's craft.

For its heart is of iron, its gleam of gold,
It is pointed to pierce and barbed to hold,
And its wonderful story is hardly told.

It is poised on a finger from sun to sun,
And it catches the glimmer of dawn begun,
And is floating in light when the day is done.

And it turns at the touch of a viewless hand,
And it swings in the air like a wizard's wand,
By the tempest whirled and the zephyr fanned.

And the sinewy finger that cannot tire
Is the lifted hush of the old church spire
That vanishes out as heaven is nigher;

And the arrow upon it the rusted vane
As true to its master as faith to fane,
That is swinging forever in sun and rain.

Right about to the North! And the trumpets blow
And the shivering air is dim with snow,
And the earth grows dumb and the brooks run slow;

And the shaggy Arctic, chilled to the bone,
Is craunching the world with a human moan,
And the clank of a chain in the frozen zone;

And the world is dead in its seamless shroud,
And the stars wink slow in the rifted cloud,
And the owl in the oak complains aloud.

But the arrow is true to the iceberg's realm,
As the rudder staunch in the ghastly whelm
With a hero by to handle the helm!

THE VANE ON THE SPIRE.

Is it welded with frost as iron with fire?
Up with a blue-jacket! Clamber the spire
And swing it around to the point of desire!

It sways to the East! And the icy rain
With the storm's "long roll" on the window pane
And a diamond point on the crystal vane.

And the cattle stand with the wind astern,
And the routes of the rain on eave and urn —
As the drops are halted and frozen in turn —

Are such pendants of wonder as cave and mine
Never gave to the gaze when the torches shine,
But right out of Heaven and half divine!

Ah, it swings due South to the zephyr's thrill!
In the yellow noon it lies as still
As a speckled trout by the drowsy mill,

While the bugle of Gabriel wakes the sod
And the beautiful life in the speechless clod,
'Till the crowded June is a smile for God!

Resurrection to-day! For the roses spoke!
Resurrection to-day! For the rugged oak
In a live green billow rolled and broke.

And the spider feels for her silken strings,
And the honey-bee hums and the world has wings,
And blent with the blue the bluebird sings.

While the cloud is ablaze with the bended bow,
And the waters white with the lilies' snow,
On the motionless arrow, all in a row,

Are four little sparrows that pipe so small
Their carol distils as the dew-drops fall,
And we only *see* they are singing at all!

Now the arrow is swung with a sweep so bold
Where the Day has been flinging his garments gold
'Till they stain the sky with a glow untold.

Ah, the cardinal point of the wind is West!
And the clouds bear down in a fleet abreast,
And the world is as still as a child at rest!

There's a binnacle light like an angry star,
And the growl of a gun with its crash and jar,
And the roll of a drum where the angels are!

And it tumbles its freight on the dancing grain,
And it beats into blossom the buds again,
And it brightens a world baptized in rain,

And it gladdens the earth as it drifts along,
And the meadow is green and the corn is strong,
And the brook breaks forth in the same old song!

And I looked for the arrow — it hung there yet,
With the drops of the rain its barb was wet,
And the sun shone out in a crimson set;

And behold, aloft in the ruddy shine
Where the crystal water again was wine,
And it hallowed the dart like a touch divine!

    Under the sun and under the moon,
    Silver at midnight, golden at noon,
Could Dian have lost it out of her hair?
Phœbús's quiver have shaken it there?
That wonderful arrow sweeping the air!

DECORATION DAY.

O H, be dumb all ye clouds
    As the dead in their shrouds,
Let your pulses of thunder die softly away,
    Ye have nothing to do
    But to drift round the blue,
For the emerald world grants a furlough to-day!

    Bud, blossom, and flower
    All blended in shower,
In the grandest and gentlest of rains shall be shed
    On the acres of God
    With their billows of sod
Breaking breathless and beautiful over the dead!

    They do flush the broad land
    With the flower-laden hand,

Drift the dimples of graves with the colors of even;
    Where a BOY IN BLUE dreams
    A " Forget-me-not" gleams —
No rain half so sweet ever fell out of Heaven!

    From no angel was caught
    The magnificent thought
To pluck daisies and roses, those *bravest* of things,—
    For they stand all the while
    In their graves with a smile,—
And to strew with live fragrance dead lions and kings!

    It was somebody born,
    It was Rachel forlorn.
'T was the love they named Mary, the trust they called Ruth;
    'T was a *woman* who told
    That the blossoms unfold
A defiance to death and a challenge for truth;
    That the violet's eye,
    Though it sleep, by and by
Shall watch out the long age in the splendor of youth.

Ah, she hallowed the hour
When she gathered the flower;
When she said, "This shall emblem the fame of
my brave!"
When she thought, "This shall borrow
"Brighter azure to-morrow;"
When she laid it to-day on the crest of a grave!

A WINTER PSALM.

A SONG for the meek old Mountains — the
Mountains grand and strong,
That lifted winter clear of earth all spring and
summer long,
And made it gay with evergreen, and then with
one accord
They shouldered the snows in silence and stood
before the Lord.

They did it for the roses' sake — that robins might
be born,
And Indian gold might flash along the rank and
file of corn,
And sheafy wigwam everywhere lift up its tawny
cone,
And Rachel sing the harvest home where harvest
moons had shone;

They did it for the little graves — bade flowers
    and children say,
We'll smile together by and by and fill the world
    with May!

Well done for the grim old Mountains! And well
    for the King who laid
Upon their shoulders stout and brave his gold and
    crimson blade.
'T was meet that the princely Morning, with ban-
    ners all unfurled,
Should knight them with his royal touch across
    the blushing world.

As softly as on mountain air beatitudes were
    shed,
As gently as the lilies bud among the words He
    said,
So did the dear old Mountains lay the sparkling
    winter down
Upon the poor dumb bosom of a world so bare and
    brown —

So noiselessly and silently, such radiance and rest!
As if a snowy wing should fold upon a sparrow's breast.

Far through the dim uncertain air, as still as asters blow,
The downy drowsy feet untold tread out the world we know;
Upon the pine's green fingers set, flake after flake they land,
And flicker with a feeble light amid the shadowy band;
Upon the meadows broad and brown where maids and mowers sung;
Upon the meadows gay with gold the dandelions flung;
Upon the farmyard's homely realm, on ricks and rugged bars,
Till riven oak and strawy heap were domes and silver spars;
The cottage was an eastern dream with alabaster eaves,
And lilacs growing round about with diamonds for leaves;

The well-sweep gray above the roof a silver accent
    stood,
And silver willows wept their way to meet a silver
    wood;
The russet groves had blossomed white and budded
    full with stars,
The fences were in uniform, the gate-posts were
    hussars;
The chimneys were in turbans all, with plumes of
    crimson smoke,
And the costly breaths were silver when the laugh-
    ing children spoke;
And gem and jewel everywhere along the tethers
    strung
Where mantling roses once had climbed and morn-
    ing glories swung.
So through the dim, uncertain air, as still as asters
    blow,
The downy drowsy feet untold tread out the world
    we know.

The glimmer of the violet's eye goes out beneath
    their tread,

White silence lines the ringing street and drifts
around the dead,
But more than all they trample out the crooked
paths of men,
And make the stained and wrinkled world all clean
and young again!
The summer rain hath won sweet song from many
a tuneful soul
Since God did paint day's alphabet upon the cloudy
scroll,
But who for the snow shall give us one grand
angelic psalm,
The beautiful feet of the snow — the feet so pure
and calm?

Thanks be to God for winter time! That bore the
Mayflower up,
To pour amid New England snows the treasures
of its cup,
To fold them in its icy arms, those sturdy Pilgrim
sires,
And weld an iron brotherhood around their Christ-
mas fires!

Thanks be to God for winter time! How strong
    the pulses play,
And ah, the pulses of the bells are not less sweet
    than they!
Dear heart of winter, throb again with old melo-
    dious beat,
Around thy glow for ever heard the play of
    childhood's feet,
Worn smooth and beautiful the Rock where later
    Pilgrims come
To harvest all their loves and hopes around the
    hearth of home!

SAILING OF COLUMBUS.

IMMORTAL they made it, if anything could,
   That wonderful day when Columbus's brood
Slipped silently out from the earth's azure eaves,—
Like a flock of young swallows when summer-time
   leaves,
And plumed up their pinions and parted the blue,
And the sky was unrent, and the trinity through!
Shook off the old world and shook out for the new!
Were they shrived ere they went? Were their
   sins all forgiven?
For they 'll flutter their wings at the windows of
   Heaven!
Hark! The Admiral's hail: "World ahoy! Whither
   bound?"
And the answer comes back on a breaker of sound,
And the flag of the Andes in fire is unfurled,
And Niagara's thunder of welcome is hurled,
"We 're at anchor, your honor! It is Liberty's
   World!"

THE CHRYSALIS.

A COFFIN gray and spotted with gold
   With a mulberry leaf for bier,
And silken shroud with a silver fold,
   On a shelf is lying near.

They say when April comes to the door,
   And the blue-eyed foundlings wake,
The humble thing that was dead before
   From its silken sleep shall break;

A folio flower, in duplicate done,
   Like the face in the eyes of a wife,
Two leaves shall open slow in the sun
   With a dissyllabic life.

THE FLAG.

OH, glimpse of clear heaven,
    Artillery riven,
The Fathers' old fallow God seeded with stars,
    Thy furrows were turning
    When plowshares were burning,
And the half of each bout is redder than Mars!

    Flaunt forever thy story
    Oh, wardrobe of glory!
Where the Fathers laid down their mantles of blue,
    And challenged the ages,—
    Oh, grandest of gages!—
In covenant solemn, eternal, and true.

THE HERO OF NEW HAMBURG.

THE grandest charge of cavalry
   That ever was seen or sung
The solitary trooper made,
   Who spoke in the Latin tongue.
Bring out your Roman rider
   Who carried the Gulf by storm,
And the dumb earth closed forever
   And shrouded his vanished form;
Sowed like the seed that has fallen,
   'Mid the multitude's acclaim,
How it blossomed through the ages
   Till it ripened into fame!

I can *match* your daring rider,
   Tell the Roman not to wait!
There's another hard behind him
   Drawing rein at Glory's gate!

Comes the deathless Engineer,
   Clears the ages at a leap,
Crowds the flock of years together
   As a shepherd folds his sheep —
Right across historic pages
   With a clatter and a clank,
Craunches time to scintillations,
     Closes up the broken rank,
     Smites the Roman in the flank!

Nevermore shall mighty boatswain
   Pipe all hands with panting fire;
Sweep thy soul, oh lion-hearted,
   As Apollo swept the lyre!
Loose thy grasp, immortal Brakeman!
   Flinging free the iron rein,
Earth! be taught articulation,
     Learn by heart the dread refrain,
     Jar and thunder back again!
Dare ye quench Elijah's chariot,
   Lightning touch and Titan tread?
Abandon every wheel and axle,
   Furl forever, flags of red!

Halt him not with battle lantern,
   Show a light as white as day!
Let him pass, O signal stations,
   His for aye "THE RIGHT OF WAY!"

Flanked by rugged rock and river,
   Death and double side by side —
Hand upon the mighty bridle,
   See the gallant horseman ride;
See the ponderous creature coming,
   Sway and swing along the track,
Brave postilion in the saddle,
   Flying chambers at his back —
Chambers bright with hope and dreaming,
   Chambers dark with terror dire —
Chambers? Altars for a demon's
   Dreadful sacrifice of fire!

On it comes, the sinewed being,
   With its rider grand and calm,
Watch and heart keep steady beating
   Like an old long-meter psalm!

Stolen out of Eastern story,
   Garbed in brass, this Arab's dream
Plunges through the tunneled thunder,
   Cambric needle through a seam;
Flickering dimly in the distance,
   Flaring broadly into sight
With his dawn of human making,
   Break of day in heart of night!
Grumbling in the lairs of mountains,
   Roaring down the valley broad,
Rounding out a sturdy headland,
   Blazing like a Grecian god!

Now this rider strangely changes —
   Touch him with a wizard's wand,
He shall seem a wondrous gunner
   With the lanyard in his hand;
'Taking sight across the kingdoms,
   Cloud by day, by night a flame,
He trains his winged artillery,
     At a target taking aim,
     Sure to watch if not to pray,

Drift December, blossom May,
At a target night and day,
Full a thousand miles away
Taking aim!

Columned smokes built high and mighty
   Colonnade the dome of night;
Kindles like a face the dial
   With the bursts of furnace light,
And the rider at his window,
   Watching with a pleasant smile,
Sees the friendly world to meet him
   Coming down the track the while,
   Sixty seconds make a mile!

Halt him on your rounds, ye Angels,
   Swinging wide the lights of God!
Watchmen, flash afar the signal,
   "Death is waiting down the road!"
Halt him with your dropping lanterns,
   Shed like stars from ripened sky —
Halt him, glances red and lurid,
   Glaring like an angry eye!

All run down the clocks of danger,
  Dials with the sunshine passed!
Come the keen shrill cry and challenge,
  Death and Duty meet at last!
Now transfigured stands the rider,
  Flinging down his rude disguise,
Sturdy hand upon the bridle,
  Telling how a hero dies.
" Hold her hard," he bade the brakeman,
  Clutched the monster by the throat
Till the bell with sudden clangor
  Tolled as if the sexton smote.
And the grand rebellious creature
  Plunged into the empty air,
Swung him out to resurrection
  Clad in Fame's immortal wear!
Born alive to song and story
  Comes this Engineer again,
Comes this man to plead for honor
  As the gage of kingly men;
Pleading that the grace of dying
  Is the rarest grace of all;
That the earth's sublimest heroes
  Never heard a bugle call;

That the clock of Christ's own ages
    Never yet had sounded " one,"
If this planet's grandest jewel
    Had been nothing but a crown!

To his steed they *lashed* Mazeppa,
    Smithfield clanked with martyrs' chains,
But this man, bound round with honor,
    Gathering up the iron reins,
Free as Chimborazo's eagle
    Flaps his pinion over head,
Charged forlorn at utter danger
    As if Death itself were dead!
Halt him not with battle lantern,
    Show a light as white as day!
Let him pass, O signal stations,
    His for aye " THE RIGHT OF WAY!"

THE GOSPEL OF THE OAK.

WAR TIME, 1863.

UP to the Sun magnificently near,
   The Lord did build a Californian oak,
And took no Sabbath in the thousandth year,
   But builded on until it bravely broke
Into that realm wherein the morning light
Walks to and fro upon the top of night!
Around that splendid shaft no hammers rang,
Nor giants wrought nor truant angels sang,
But gentle winds and painted birds did bear
Its corner-stones of glory through the air;
Grand volumes green rolled up like cloudy weather,
And birds and stars went in and out together;
When Day on errands from the Lord came down,
It stepped from Heaven to that leafy crown!

God's mighty mast with all its sails unfurled,
That ought to make a Druid of the world.

Some Vandal girdled with a zone of death,
A life of ages perished in a breath!
Good night, Live Oak! Proud admiral, farewell!
The world has wailed when meaner monarchs
    fell!

The year went on, and with it marched sublime,
Month after Month, the journeymen of Time.
Then came the May, such wings as angels wear,
Buds in her hands and blossoms in her hair:
Above that oak she shook her flowing sleeves—
The poor dead tree laughed out with living leaves!
Thank God! Too vast, too grand to die forlorn
It lived right on! Brave heart of oak, good
    morn!

I'd be a Roman for the omen grand
That thunders on the left through all the land—
God and the Fathers' tree forever stand!
Oh, growth immortal, reddened in the rain
That beats out hearts as tempests beat the grain,
All wrongs died out like breath upon a blade,
A hunted world fled panting to thy shade—

Thy roots have searched earth's bosom all around,
Felt out the graves that make it holy ground —
Like living hands with love and faith been laid
In benediction on the sleeping dead!

THE TWO JOHNS.

Do you think we are crushed out of loving and
        living
By the fall of a clod, when the planet is giving
To the delicate foot of an ounce of a wren,
And then surges right up as she lifts it again?
Oh, Gibeon's Sun! He is yet under orders,
You can halt him to-day on death's gloomy bor-
        ders;
Bid brave thoughts and grand deeds the dead
        Joshua play —
"Stand still, mighty Sun!" and the blaze shall
        obey.

Take a page of blind JOHN that angels have
        tramped
Till it looks as if stars broke ranks and encamped —

So strown about with fine gold from Ormus and
 Ind
That you wonder how angels could ever have
 sinned,
When old English brocade at such exquisite cost,
To tell the strange story of " Paradise Lost "
Did bankrupt the bard, so nothing remained
To tell us the story of Eden " Regained."
Look down on the page and declare if you can
What business the grave-digger had with the
 man!
Dare Hamlet's own sexton, or one of his tribe,
Lay an ounce of dead clay upon Cromwell's old
 scribe?
Those angels of his — they have put them to
 rout!
Those angels of his — they have lifted him out!
As free of the ages as the winds of the waves,
And abolished that gloomy old fashion of graves!

In this Christendom's realm, in some year of our
 Lord,
Men attacked with a fagot the soul of a word;

Ah, hundreds of years Christmas carols were sung,
Ere they dwelt in this world and spoke in our
    tongue
Who groped in the ashes where martyrs were
    chained,
If perchance a live coal of the embers remained,
And they blew it to life in the name of the kings,
And the books of this MILTON all took to their
    wings
Like his own bird-of-paradise, crimson and gold,
And the princes grew warm as the ashes grew cold!
'T was as if some old Vandal should vainly aspire
To strike David dumb by just burning his lyre;—
The books played Elijah—left their mantle be-
    hind,
And it fell and unfurled, till it kindled mankind.

And that Prince of all Pilgrims, the other twin
    JOHN,—
He will walk in his sleep till the ages are gone;
Blow softly, oh Angel! Let him slumber right on.
With the swing of the sledge for the music of flutes
He beat up the world for celestial recruits;—

He dreamed himself through to the "Beautiful Gate,"
With "Christian" for comrade and "Mercy" to wait.
Time's sentries cry "halt!" Hark the sturdy reply:
Oh, be lifted, ye gates, for old BUNYAN goes by!
Pass on, grand crusader! Hearts warm to thy name —
Good night to thy form but good morn to thy fame!

BEAUTIFUL "MAY."

OH, have you not seen on some morning in June,
    When the flowers were in tears and the forest in tune,
And the billows of dawn broke bright on the air,
On the breast of the brightest a star clinging there?
Some Sentinel Star, not ready to set,
Forgetting to wane and watching there yet?
How you gazed on that vision of beauty awhile,
How it wavered till won by the light of God's smile,
How it passed through the portals of pearl like a bride,
How it paled as it passed, and the Morning Star died!
The sky was all blushes, the world was all bliss,
And the prayer of your heart, " Be my ending like this!"

So my beautiful MAY passed away from life's even,
So the blush of her being was blended with Heaven;
So the bird of my bosom fluttered up to the dawn —
Ah, a window was open — my darling was gone —
A truant from time, from tears, and from sin,
For the angel on watch took the wanderer in!
When she warbles to me the New Song that she sings,
I shall know her again notwithstanding her wings,
By those eyes full of heaven — by the light on her hair —
And the smile she wore here she will surely wear there!

THE NORTHERN LIGHTS.

To claim the Arctic came the Sun,
　　With banners of the burning zone;
Unrolled upon their airy spars
They froze beneath the light of stars;
And there they float, those streamers old,
Those Northern Lights, forever cold!

INDIAN SUMMER.

THEN past the yellow regiments of corn
   There came an Indian Maiden, autumn born,
And June returned and held her by the hand,
And led Time's smiling Ruth through all the land;
A veil of golden air was o'er her flung,
The South wind whispered and the robins sung.

THE SHATTERED RAINBOW.

WHEN blazed the trinket of the cloud abroad,
    The bent and broken jewelry of God,
That fragment of a ring — its *other* part
Was lost, I dreamed, within the forest's heart.
And when October came with eager clasp,
The jewel shivered in his frosty grasp
And showered the maples with celestial red —
The oaks were sunsets though the days were dead,
The green was gold, the willows drooped in wine,
The ash was fire, the humblest shrub divine.

FIRE AND WATER.

MAGNIFICENT AGE! When water and fire,
   The lamb and the lion, together conspire,
And the atom of rain the robins are drinking
Can set the dull iron to throbbing and thinking.
It enters the heart of a ship in her sleep —
There's a cloud on the sky — a wake on the deep —
There's a soul in the oak that would kindle a
   king,
And she crashes away without lifting a wing!

Take the old "Franklin press," where the dead
   were laid out,
And the printer in mourning went plodding about,
Till a creak and a groan broke the pages' repose,
And the specters in sheets, one by one, in their
   clothes,
To a late resurrection reluctantly rose!

Now inspire the machine with flood and with flame,
And call it a brother and give it a name!
It comes down to the work with a will and a clank,
Strikes the types in the face and the wrongs in the flank;
In the flash of an eye the creature has caught
And kindled and glowed with the life of the thought!
Stand clear of the thing! It is nearing the brink
Where a being unborn is beginning to think!
It flutters its plumage, and drifts the world white—
And it snows down the ages its treasures of light!
It flutters its plumage — this marvelous bird,—
Put a lock on your heart and beware of the word
That *it* pulses abroad, for creation has heard.
The lightning's vernacular thunder, is dumb,
The bolts strike the word, talk English and come;
The surge tells the billow, the breakers repeat,
Till the waves of the sea wash the words to your feet,
Dry-shod from the anchorage down in the brine,
Swung up by the cable, a creature divine.

FIRE AND WATER.

See the forge's first-born with its sinews of steel,
A nerve at each lever and axle and wheel,
All ready to fly and just ready to feel,
Pluck out of its caskets great handfuls of power,
The flocks of mankind all shorn in an hour
And the fleeces just granted this Thing for a dower,
To weave as it went a wonderful robe
To be flung on the sea and apparel the globe!
Born last of a furnace and first of a dream,
It learned elocution from eagles that scream;
Lo, the flash of its eye as it kindles the track
With the wild at its front and the world at its
    back!

I beg you to think of the pioneer's stroke
That the sleep of the wilderness lazily broke:
The blow of that axe was the beat of the clock
That timed the whole route from Plymouth's gray
    rock.
Now you bend your ear down to the marvelous
    wire,
That orbit man strung for articulate fire,—
For globe and for lightning a nerve.and a lyre,—

And you start at a grander chronometer's beat,
As strong and distinct as a step in the street,
Away there in the desert, away here in the mart,
So near that you think it the beat of your heart,
When the silver-bound laurel lay fast in its place,
And they gave to the work its finishing grace,
And you heard with your soul, when the hammer
    let fall,
Drove the golden spike home for good and for all!
That couplet of iron — match the line if you can,
The grandest of epics yet uttered by man —
Has heaved up the sky, reft the blue from the
    green!
See the western horizon sublimely careen
To let in the East and its kingdoms between!

"*ATLANTIC.*"

Ay, build her long and narrow and deep!
  She shall cut the sea with a scimetar's sweep,
Whatever betides and whoever may weep!

Bring out the red wine! Lift the glass to the lip!
With a roar of great guns, and a " Hip! hip!
" Hurrah!" for the craft, we will christen the ship!

Dash a draught on the bow! Ah, the spar of
    white wood
Drips into the sea till it colors the flood
With the very own double and symbol of blood!

Now out with the name of the monarch gigantic
That shall queen it so grandly when surges are
    frantic!
Child of fire and of iron, God save the ATLANTIC!

All freighted with power below and above,
The heart of a fiend and the wing of a dove—
Tumble in the brave cargo of life and of love!

Good for a thousand souls! Hustle them in!
Your mother and mine shall the census begin;
Then tell off the children too little to sin!

With furnace of fire and forest of mast,
She can conquer the calm and rally the blast;
But fuel is costly! Coal-heavers avast!

Ah, those ebony heaps that cumber the hold
Can never be reckoned in silver and gold—
Ten lives to the ton, and an anguish untold!

Alas for the lack of a handful of coals;
Alas for the ship that is haunted with souls;
Alas for the bell that eternally tolls!

All aboard, my fine fellows! " Up anchor!" the
    word—
Ah, never again shall that order be heard,
For two worlds will be mourning ye gone to a third!

To the trumpet of March wild gallops the sea;
The white-crested troopers are under the lee —
Old World and New World and Soul-World are
    three

Great garments of rain wrap the desolate night;
Sweet Heaven disastered is lost to the sight;
" ATLANTIC," crash on in the pride of thy might!
With thy look-out's dim cry, " One o'clock, and
    all right!"

Ho, down with the hatches! The seas come
    aboard!
All together they come, like a passionate word
Like pirates that put every soul to the sword!

Their black flag all abroad makes murky the air,
But the ship parts the night as a maiden her
    hair—
Through and through the thick gloom, from land
    here to land there,
Like the shuttle that weaves for a mourner to
    wear!

Good night, proud " ATLANTIC!" One tick of
    the clock,
And a staggering craunch and a shivering shock —
'T is the flint and the steel! 'T is the ship and
    the rock!

Deathless sparks are struck out from the bosoms
    of girls,
From the stout heart of manhood in scintillant
    whirls,
Like the stars of the Flag when the banner un-
    furls!

What hundreds went up unto God in their sleep!
What hundreds in agony baffled the deep —
Nobody to pray and nobody to weep!

Alas for the flag of the single " White Star,"
With light pale and cold as the woman's hands are
Who, froze in the shrouds, flashed her jewels
    afar,
Lost her hold on the world, and then clutched at a
    spar!

God of mercy and grace ! How the bubbles come
    up
With souls from the revel, who stayed not to sup;
Death drank the last toast, and then shattered the
    cup !

Who crushed these poor hearts that wild terror
    environ ? —
Atlantic of water ? Atlantic of iron ?
The den where they bearded the granite old
    lion ?
The God of the sparrows ? A breath from Mount
    Zion ?

Bring the World into court ! Bid the verdict be
    given !
" To this true word we render, resistlessly driven,
" And so say we all — NOT GUILTY, 'fore Heaven ! "

Poor handful of carbon ! Call humanity's roll
For the fellow who thought, " Ah, how costly is
    coal ! "
He loses who bids *any* price for his soul !

And Christ died for this man — this pitiful creature!
Made like the noblest in fashion and feature —
Saint John the Belov'd and the Wilderness Preacher!

Too sordid for soul and too subtle for sod,
Let us lock out of heart the poor animate clod,
And leave the new Cain and his brother with God!

In the clash of the leaves of the frantic woods,
And the turbulent whirl of the angry floods,
And the rumble and roar of the cloudy broods,

In the height of the storm, you have sometimes heard
The melodious voice of an unseen bird,
And so clear and so brave that your heart was stirred;

It seemed to be Faith set anew to a song,
That the weakest of things need never fear wrong
If they only believe in the true and the strong.

In that bitterer storm, when the plunge of the wreck
Tossed the white forms at will that were strewing the deck,
As the foam-flakes are tossed on a war-horse's neck,

And men growing grim in their hunger for life,
And husband in frenzy abandoning wife
To struggle alone in the desperate strife,

Then a voice brave and young rose sweet through the din:
" Lend a hand ! I 'm alone with a lifetime to win ! "
'T was the song of an angel rebuking the sin.

Then the brute that 's in men slunk back to its lair —
Strong fingers were wound in the boy's curly hair —
" Pass the lad right along ! My chance he shall share ! "

THE CAVALRY CHARGE

HARK! the rattling roll of the musketeers,
 And the ruffled drums and the rallying cheers,
And the rifles burn with a keen desire
Like the crackling whips of a Hemlock fire,
And the singing shot and the shrieking shell
And the splintered fire of the shattered hell,
And the great white breaths of the cannon smoke
As the growling guns by batteries spoke;
And the ragged gaps in the walls of blue
Where the iron surge rolled heavily through,
That the Colonel builds with a breath again
As he cleaves the din with his " Close up, men!"
And the groan torn out from the blacken'd lips,
And the prayer doled slow with the crimson drips,
And the beaming look in the dying eye
As under the cloud the STARS go by,

"But his soul marched on," the Captain said,
For the Boy in Blue can never be dead!

And the troopers sit in their saddles all
Like statues carved in an ancient hall,
And they watch the whirl from their breathless
   ranks,
And their spurs are close to the horses' flanks,
And the fingers work of the sabre hand—
Oh, to bid them live, and to make them grand!
And the bugle sounds to the charge at last,
And away they plunge and the front is passed!
And the jackets blue grow red as they ride,
And the scabbards too, that clank by their side,
And the dead soldiers deaden the strokes iron shod
As they gallop right on o'er the plashy red sod—
Right into the cloud all spectral and dim,
Right up to the guns black-throated and grim,
Right down on the hedges bordered with steel,
Right through the dense columns, then "right
   about wheel!"
Hurrah! A new swath through the harvest again!
Hurrah for the Flag! To the battle, Amen!

FORT DEARBORN.

THE OLD — *October 8th,* '71.   THE NEW — *October 8th,* '73.

BORN of the prairie and the wave — the blue
    sea and the green,
A city of the Occident, CHICAGO lay between;
Dim trails upon the meadow, faint wakes upon
    the main,
On either sea a schooner and a canvas-covered
    wain.

I saw a dot upon the map, and a house-fly's filmy
    wing —
They said 't was Dearborn's picket-flag when
    Wilderness was king;
I heard the reed-bird's morning song — the Indian's awkward flail —
The rice tattoo in his rude canoe like a dash of
    April hail —

The beaded grasses' rustling bend — the swash of
    the lazy tide,
Where ships shake out the salted sails and navies
    grandly ride!

I heard the Block-house gates unbar, the column's
    solemn tread,
I saw the Tree of a single leaf its splendid foliage
    shed
To wave awhile that August morn above the
    column's head;
I heard the moan of muffled drum, the woman's
    wail of fife,
The Dead March played for Dearborn's men just
    marching out of life,
The swooping of the savage cloud that burst upon
    the rank
And struck it with its thunderbolt in forehead and
    in flank,
The spatter of the musket-shot, the rifles' whistling
    rain —
The sand-hills drift round hope forlorn that never
    marched again!

L

I SEE in tasseled rank and file the regiments of
 corn,
Their bending sabres, millions strong, salute the
 summer morn ;
The harvest-fields, as round and red as full-grown
 harvest-moon,
That fill the broad horizons up with mimic gold of
 noon ;
I count a thousand villages like flocks in pastures
 grand,
I hear the roar of caravans through all the blessèd
 land —
CHICAGO grasps the ripened year and holds it in
 her hand!
"Give us this day our daily bread!" the planet's
 Christian prayer ;
CHICAGO, with her open palm, makes answer
 everywhere!

I hear the march of multitudes who said the map
 was wrong —
They drew the net of Longitude and brought it
 right along,

And swung a great Meridian Line across the
   Foundling's breast,
And the city of the Occident was neither East
   nor West!
Her charter is no dainty thing of parchment and
   of pen,
But written on the prairie's page by full a million
   men;
They use the ploughshare and the spade, and end-
   less furrows run,
Line after line the record grows, and yet is just
   begun;
They rive the pines of Michigan and give them to
   the breeze —
The keel-drawn Charter's draft inscribes the
   necklace of the seas,
'T is rudely sketched in anthracite, engraved on
   copper plate,
And traced across the Continent to Ophir's Golden
   Gate!
The Lord's Recording Angel holds the Charter in
   his hand —
He seals it on the sea, and he signs it on the land!

Unroll the royal Charter now! It "marches" with the West,
Embossed along its far frontier, Sierra's silver crest;
Along its hither border shines a sacred crystal chain:
God cursed of old the weedy ground, but never cursed the main,
As free to-day from earthly sin as Eden's early rain!

"I found a Rome of common clay," Imperial Cæsar cried;
"I left a Rome of marble!" No other Rome beside!
The ages wrote their autographs along the sculptured stone —
The golden eagles flew abroad — Augustan splendors shone —
They made a Roman of the world! They trailed the classic robe,
And flung the Latin toga around the naked globe!

"I found Chicago wood and clay," a mightier Kaiser said,
Then flung upon the sleeping mart his royal robes of red,
And temple, dome, and colonnade, and monument and spire,
Put on the crimson livery of dreadful Kaiser Fire!
The stately piles of polished stone were shattered into sand,
And madly drove the dread simoon, and snowed them on the land!
And rained them till the sea was red, and scorched the wings of prayer!
Like thistle-down ten thousand homes went drifting through the air,
And dumb Dismay, walked hand in hand with frozen-eyed Despair!
CHICAGO vanished in a cloud — the towers were storms of sleet,
Lo! ruins of a thousand years along the spectral street!
The night burned out between the days! The ashen hoar-frost fell,

As if some demon set ajar the bolted gates of hell,
And let the molten billows break the adamantine
    bars,
And roll the smoke of torment up to smother out
    the stars!
The low, dull growl of powder-blasts just dotted
    off the din,
As if they tolled for perished clocks the time that
    might have been!
The thunder of the fiery surf roared human accents
    dumb;
The trumpet's clangor died away a wild bee's
    drowsy hum,
And breakers beat the empty world that rumbled
    like a drum.
O cities of the Silent Land! O Graceland and
    Rosehill!
No tombs without their tenantry? The pale host
    sleeping still?
Your marble thresholds dawning red with holo-
    caustal glare,
As if the Waking Angel's foot were set upon the
    stair!

But ah, the human multitudes that marched before
    the flame,
As 'mid the Red Sea's wavy walls the ancient
    people came!
Behind, the rattling chariots! the Pharaoh of Fire!
The rallying volley of the whips—the jarring of
    the tire!
Looked round, and saw the homeless world as
    dismal as a pyre—
Looked up, and saw God's blessèd Blue a firma-
    ment so dire!
As in the days of burning Troy, when Virgil's
    hero fled,
So gray and trembling pilgrims found some younger
    feet instead,
That bore them through the wilderness with bold
    elastic stride,
And Ruth and Rachel, pale and brave, in silence
    walked beside;
Those Bible girls of Judah's day did make *that*
    day sublime —
Leave life but *them*, no other loss can ever bank-
    rupt Time!

Men stood and saw their all caught up in chariots of flame —
No mantle falling from the sky they ever thought to claim,
And empty-handed as the dead, they turned away and smiled,
And bore a stranger's household gods and saved a stranger's child!
What valor brightened into shape, like statues in a hall,
When on their dusky panoply the blazing torches fall,
Stood bravely out and saw the world spread wings of fiery flight,
And not a trinket of a star to crown disastered night!

"Who runs these lines of telegraph?" A clock-tick made reply:
"'The greatest of the three' has brought this message from the sky,
"The Lord will send an Angel down to work these lines to-day!"

Charge all the batteries good and strong! Give
 GOD the right of way!
And so the swift evangels ran by telegraphic time,
And brought the cheer of Christendom from every
 earthly clime;
Celestial fire flashed round the globe, from Norway
 to Japan,
Proclaimed the MANhood of the race, the BROTHER-
 hood of man!
Then flashed a hundred engines' arms — then flew
 the lightning trains;
They had that day the right of way — gave every
 steed the reins —
The minutes came, the minutes went — the miles
 fled just the same —
And flung along October night their starry flags
 of flame!
They all were angels in disguise, from hamlet,
 field, and mart,
CHICAGO'S fire had warmed the World that had
 her woe by heart.
" Who is my neighbor?" One and all: " We see
 her signal light,

" And She our *only* neighbor now, this wild October night ! "

" I found CHICAGO wood and clay," the royal Kaiser cried,
And flung upon the sleeping mart the mantle in his pride ;
It lay awhile — he lifted it, and there beneath the robe
A city done in lithograph, the wonder of the globe ;
Where granite grain and marble heart, in strength and beauty wed,—
" I leave a mart of palaces," the haughty Kaiser said.

Now, thanks to GOD, this blessèd day, to whom all thanks belong —
The clash of silver cymbals, the rhyme of the little song —
Whose Hand did hive the golden bees that swarm the azure dome,
Whence honey-dews forever fall around this earthly home —

Did constellate the prairie sod and light it up with
 flowers —
That Hand defend from fire and flood this Prairie
 Flower of ours!
This volume of the royal West we bring in grateful gage,
We open at the frontispiece and give it to the Age,
Who wrote the word CHICAGO *twice* upon the
 title-page!

THE ISLE OF THE LONG AGO.

OH, a wonderful stream is the River Time,
  As it flows through the realm of Tears,
With a faultless rhythm and a musical rhyme,
And a broader sweep and a surge sublime
  As it blends with the ocean of Years.

II.

How the winters are drifting like flakes of snow!
  And the summers like buds between;
And the year in the sheaf — so they come and
  they go
On the River's breast with its ebb and flow,
  As they glide in the shadow and sheen.

III.

There's a magical Isle up the River Time
  Where the softest of airs are playing;
There's a cloudless sky and a tropical clime,
And a voice as sweet as a vesper chime,
  And the Junes with the roses are staying.

IV.

And the name of this Isle is the Long Ago,
    And we bury our treasures there;
There are brows of beauty and bosoms of snow—
They are heaps of dust, but we loved them so!
    There are trinkets and tresses of hair.

V.

There are fragments of song that nobody sings,
    And a part of an infant's prayer,
There's a harp unswept and a lute without strings,
There are broken vows and pieces of rings,
    And the garments that she used to wear.

VI.

There are hands that are waved when the fairy shore
    By the mirage is lifted in air;
And we sometimes hear through the turbulent roar
Sweet voices we heard in the days gone before,
    When the wind down the River is fair.

VII.

Oh, remembered for aye be the blessed Isle
    All the day of our life till night,
And when evening comes with its beautiful smile,
And our eyes are closing in slumber awhile,
    May that "GREENWOOD" of soul be in sight.

THE ROSE AND THE ROBIN.

THE yellow rose leaves falling down
  Pay golden toll to passing June,
The robin's breast of golden brown
  Is trembling with an ancient tune.

The rose will bloom another year,
  The robin and his wife will come,
But he who sees may not be here,
  And he who sings be dumb.

Thy grace be mine, oh yellow rose!
  My heart like thine its blossoms shed,
Grow fragrant to the fragrant close,
  And sweetest when I'm dead.

And so like thee I'll pay my way
  In coin that time can never rust,
And footsteps sound another day
  Though feet have turned to dust!

Thy gift be mine, oh singing bird!
   My song like thine round home and heart:
To Song, God never said the word
   " To dust return, for dust thou art!"

NOTES.

TORNADO SUNDAY.— The memorable tornado that swept over Iowa, destroying the village of Camanche and leaving across the State a broad track of death and desolation. A meeting for the relief of the sufferers was held in Chicago, and the poem was written for the occasion.

THE HERO OF NEW HAMBURG.— On the night of February 6th, 1871, an oil train was wrecked on the track near the bridge at New Hamburg, on the Hudson River Railroad. The Express train bound West ran into the wreck, the bridge took fire and fell, and twenty-one persons in the Buffalo sleeping car were killed. The Engineer, E. H. SIMMONS, remained upon his engine, doing what he could to avert the threatened disaster, and failing in this, looked death in the face, chose it to desertion, and perished at his post.

GOING HOME. — A poor disheartened emigrant returning to his Eastern home from the far West, met in the streets of La Porte, Indiana, a hearse on its way to the City of the Silent. He turned aside, halted, and, with his wife and children, watched the sad procession. The poor fellow had told his story to some one never suspected of a spark of poetry, who, as he watched the meeting from the sidewalk, said, "Well, one is going East and the other going West, but they're bound the same way after all — both going home!"

THE VANE ON THE SPIRE.— During the bitter and death-dealing days of the winter and spring of 1872 I often watched the gilded arrow that swings upon the spire of the Methodist Church. And it always had a meaning for me — sometimes sad, a few times glad, and always true. Day after day, week after week, that arrow pointed North — pointed East: *always* North, always East — like the finger of Fate. The chill winds blew; the cold storms came; there were beds of languishing; there were new-made graves. Frost, sorrow, and death ruled the air in company. And all the while, the arrow told the story.

At last there came some genial days, when flowers blossomed, birds sang, the weak grew strong, and the graves were green.

The arrow on the spire had swung round to the South; it told the story still. It was no longer the finger of Fate, but a thing of beauty — a piece of aerial jewelry. It had eloquence enough to inspire a little song, had there been anybody to write it.

FIRE AND WATER.—All being ready to connect the two grand divisions of the Union Pacific Railroad, delegations from the Atlantic and Pacific coasts met, and the last spike was driven with simple but impressive ceremonies. The tie was silver-bound laurel and the spike of Californian gold. The wires of the telegraph were so connected that the fall of the hammer was echoed at nearly the same instant in offices thousands of miles away.

"ATLANTIC."—The steamship "Atlantic," struck a rock on the morning of April 1st, 1873, and was wrecked, with a fearful sacrifice of human life. The ship was out of her course, and if any reason existed for the fatal variation it was the fear that the supply of coal was insufficient to take it into its destined port. The incident of the saving of the lad, John Hanly, awakened universal interest and sympathy.

www.ingramcontent.com/pod-product-compliance
Lightning Source LLC
Chambersburg PA
CBHW020828190426
43197CB00037B/736